Running after antelope

scott carrier

Running after antelope

COUNTERPOINT

WASHINGTON, D.C.

The antelope stories, 1963 through 1997, "Come to Stay," "Windfall,"
"The Friendly Man," "The Test," and "Carpenter," were originally
broadcast on "This American Life." "Little League Haiku" and
"Trout Stream Families" were originally broadcast on "All Things
Considered." "Hitchhike" (originally titled "My Name Is Zarko, I Will
Be Your Driver"), "Cambodia, Revisited" (originally titled "Pol Pot's
Mudfish Soup"), and "Kashmir" (originally titled "Himalayan Hell")
appeared in *Esquire*. "The Test " and "The Friendly Man" (originally
titled "Working for the Friendly Man") appeared in *Harper's Magazine*.

Library of Congress Cataloging-in-Publication Data
Carrier, Scott, 1957–
Running after antelope / Scott Carrier
p.   cm.
ISBN 1-58243-111-6 (alk. paper)
1. Carrier, Scott, 1957–   2. West (U.S.)—Biography. I. Title.
CT275.C3145 A3 2001
987'033'092—dc21
[B]   00-064442

Book design by David Bullen Design

Printed in the United States of America on acid-free paper that meets
the American National Standards Institute z39-48 Standard

COUNTERPOINT
P.O. Box 65793
Washington, D.C. 20035-5793

Counterpoint is a member of the Perseus Books Group.

10   9   8   7   6   5   4   3   2   1

For the wife and kids—
Hilary, Jessi, Milo, and Alyce

contents

I don't like work—no man does—but I like what is in the work—the chance to find yourself. Your own reality—for yourself, not for others—what no other man can ever know. They can only see the mere show, and never can tell what it really means.

JOSEPH CONRAD (Marlow in *Heart of Darkness*)

The only logical response to an animal that lives obsessed with avoiding capture is to chase it.

JOSÉ ORTEGA Y GASSETT

Running after antelope

1963

      The hunt begins at dawn, my brother pulling me out of bed onto the floor.

"Come on, come on."

I'm tying my shoes and he's out the door. Outside the fog is lifting off the grass. I'm looking for my brother but I can't even see the car in the driveway. Then he comes running from the backyard. I jump and run and catch up with him across the street in the Mander's yard, and he says, "Some animals sleep in the daytime and go out at night to eat. If we hurry we can catch them before they go back in the ground."

I believe him. I have no idea how he knows these things, but he does. He goes out and runs through our neighbors' yards and catches wild animals with his bare hands—mainly lizards, turtles and snakes. He wraps them in his shirt and brings them back to the cages in the basement so he can study them for science. He is seven years old. I am six.

I'm running along behind him, and when I lose him in the fog I follow the tracks he leaves in the dew on the grass. I catch up to him, and he's down on his hands and knees crawling through the juniper bushes in front of the Goochs' house. He says, "There's a garter snake in here. I saw it. It went right in front of me." He's crawling around breaking branches and I hear the front door open and there's our neighbor, Daisy Gooch, in her bathrobe. She looks ten feet tall and 900 years old and says, "What is going on out here?"

I say, "There's a snake in your bush."

She says, "There's no snake in my bush. You boys get out of here now," and she starts for us with her broom. We take off running. We don't need to run that far; it's not like she's going to come after us, but we keep running anyway. We jump the fence at Finn Gerholdt's house and we're on the golf course, heading toward the gully. My brother says, "I think I figured out a way to run and not get tired. It's all in how you breathe. Yesterday I ran over to the gully and down to the river and back, and I didn't get out of breath. I think I can run as far as I want."

"Like the Indians," I say.

"Yeah, like the Indians."

We have everything we need. The wilderness is unfolding in front of us.

little league haiku

It was between plays. The coach was talking to the offense in the huddle, drawing on his sketch board, reprimanding somebody for screwing up on the last play. We were standing around waiting. We were the defense, and we had no coach. We had three or four formations we'd run, but we never made a call until the last minute. I remember because I made the calls. I was the Monster Man, the free safety, the captain of the defense, and I'd often call one formation as the offense broke huddle and then stand back and wait until everyone was set, the quarterback going through his count, and then call another formation, just so everything would change shape right before the ball was snapped. This added the elements of surprise and chaos to our attack. It made the offense respect and fear us, and often their plays crumbled under the disorder we caused.

The coach was in the offensive huddle, the sun was going down, and the practice was coasting to an end. We, the Highland Mighty Mite defense, were standing around quietly, minds empty, like twelve-year-old desperadoes waiting for a train. I was standing there spacing out with everyone else, and then I had this new feeling: I was conscious of being inside a shell, and looking out at the world like my uniform and even my body were just protective packaging. I was in love with the air, the smell of the grass, the warm light in the cottonwood trees at the edge of the field. I remember looking out at Bruce Seymour, our big defensive end who had already reached puberty. He had his helmet tipped up, and his hair was all sweaty, and he was gnawing on his mouthpiece. He turned and looked at me, and I wanted to say to him, "Do you feel it?" But I didn't know what "it" was.

I called a huddle and said, "We're going to do something different this time. We're going to line up in a six-three, but as they get set I'm going to say a haiku, and I want you guys to start moving around, dance around, stand on your head, do whatever you want. We'll kill them. Ready, break!"

The offense came out of their huddle, and we went into a six-three, and just as the quarterback started his count I yelled, "The wind brings dry leaves, enough to build a fire." And my defense stood up and looked at each other and looked at me and didn't do anything. The coach blew his whistle and yelled, "What's going on? What's the problem?"

I said, "We're running a haiku."

He said, "A what?"

"A haiku," I said. "We learned it today in school. 'The wind brings dry leaves, enough to build a fire.'"

"Why," he said, "would you ever want to do that?"

"It was just an idea," I said. "It didn't really work out like I thought it would. I'm ready to move on, if you are."

condor bones

They have come down from the mountain and they are not talking to each other. In the pole tent in base camp below Alpamayo, the water is boiling for dinner. I'm making noodle soup and coca tea, as this is all the food we have left. Jenkins, Wyatt and Mitsunaga are reading. My brother wants me to teach him some Spanish.

"*Huesos del condor. Los quiero huesos del condor.*" I'm telling him bones of the condor, trying to make it simple. "*¿Donde estan?* Over there is *ayah*, usually with a hand signal. *En las montanas*, up in the mountains. *La selva*, the jungle, oriental." He's paying attention, repeating, trying to memorize.

They've come down from the mountain and they didn't get to the top. For two days they tried the northwest ridge, and then spent the third day on the north face where Mitsunaga fell fifty feet, cartwheeling down a coulair, and Jenkins held him without being anchored into the mountain. It was very steep, on snow, rock and ice—nineteen thousand feet on a twenty-thousand-foot peak—much higher than they had ever been before and much farther away from home. They got scared and bivouacked in a snow cave and argued into the night.

They had grown up together, gone to the same schools, played on the same teams; the differences among them had gone unnoticed until this mountain in Peru scared them. All were twenty-one years old and were beginning different phases of their lives. Wyatt, short of stature but incredibly strong, wanted to be a professional climbing guide. He wouldn't admit to being afraid, as he understood very well that freaking out at nineteen thousand feet was a bad idea. He needed this peak to add to his resumé, and he wanted to keep going. Jenkins, tall and also very strong, was the son of a federal judge. He planned on becoming a scholar who also climbed mountains, as these were both noble pursuits. He was afraid but wouldn't admit it. Still, he wanted to continue. Jenkins and Wyatt together had climbed many mountains and, though he had often been afraid, they had always gotten to the top. Mitsunaga was the least experienced climber of the four. He was newly married, starting law school in the fall, and was thinking about nothing except getting down and getting home. My brother, who has the strongest will of anyone I've ever met and rarely gives up on anything, was deeply frightened and sided with Mitsunaga—all of them had chosen the wrong route. The mountain was more than they had expected. It wasn't worth dying for.

That evening, in between arguments, my brother watched a condor ride a thermal up the face of the mountain. He was looking down on it for five thousand vertical feet, and, when the condor was flying at the same level, they looked each other in the eye. Then he watched it from below as it went up another thousand feet and flew off over the top of the mountain.

The next morning they all decided to come back to base camp to get some more food. But there is no more food in base camp. And they're so hungry and mean-spirited that they think I ate everything; but, really, they took the good stuff—the sardines, the sugar and the butter—and ate it while they were climbing. To get even I tell them the story of the best meal I'd ever had.

"I was hitchhiking through Montreal, coming from Alaska, going to Miami, and this woman driving a Volvo picked me up and asked if she could cook dinner for me. She said her husband was on call at the hospital and that she didn't like to eat alone. She was in her late forties or early fifties, with quick, delicate eyes, a hypnotic voice, a Scandinavian accent, and her left hand had a knife scar running sideways across all her fingers.

"We went to her house and she asked me to cut up the vegetables. She got out some pans and lit a cigarette and made some coffee. She stood close to me and asked me where I was from and where I was going. She wanted to know everything.

"And then, as I was peeling potatoes, she came up and put her arms around me, put her head on my shoulder and smelled my hair and my sweater.

"The first course was potato salad with parsley and vinegar; then came sliced tomatoes with grated parmesan and white wine; then shrimp and salmon with lemon and red wine; followed by prime rib with a sweet barbecue sauce; followed by a snifter of cognac.

"After dinner, she showed me where I could sleep in a bedroom in the attic, and she said goodnight. But sometime in the middle of the night she came into my room, naked. I opened my eyes and saw her standing in the dark; she got in bed and whispered, in German, while we made love."

Jenkins says, "You made that up."

I say, "Maybe some of it."

The next day we leave base camp and walk down to a village at 12,000 feet. We buy canned sardines at the little store and spend the evening drinking beer, lying on the grass outside, watching the old matron as she bakes bread for us in an adobe oven shaped like a beehive.

As it gets dark, the light from the fire coming out of the door of the oven is the only light in the village. We lie back looking at the stars, which, in the Andes, are all as bright as planets. The old woman is standing in front of the oven staying warm, watching the bread, and my brother walks over and stands next to her.

After a minute he turns and says, "*Pardoname, ¿sabe usted donde podria encontrar los huesos de un condor?*"

"*¿Como?*" she says.

My brother says it again, and again she says, "*¿Como?*"

"*Huesos, del condor,*" he says. "I want to find some condor bones."

No, she shakes her head, no.

1982

My brother is a master's student in the biology department at the University of Utah. He works in Dr. Dennis Bramble's laboratory in the basement of the building. He's asked me to help him with an experiment. He shows me the inside of the lab's freezer, full of dead animals—roadkill he's picked up or animals he's had to kill for science. When he's ready, he takes the animals out of the freezer and puts them in the beetle box—a big, wooden chest on the floor. The beetles eat the flesh and cartilage and sinew off the bones, and then he has clean bones. Then he measures the bones—by size and shape, by weight, by finding their center, by bending them until they break, and so on. He's studying to be a vertebrate morphologist.

For the experiment we walk over to the football stadium, which is empty except for us. He fastens a styrofoam cup over my mouth. The cup has a wireless microphone inside of it. He straps another microphone to my right ankle. Then he says, "O.K., run around the track. Run a mile."

I run four laps and it is not easy. I'm out of shape from smoking too much and I tell my brother I'm sorry. He says, "That's O.K. That's why I asked you. We need data from bad runners."

I ask him what he's doing, and he says, "We, Dennis and I, are studying how animals breathe when they run. When quadrapeds gallop—animals like horses and dogs and cats—they have to inhale every time they stretch out in their stride, and then exhale when they come forward with their back legs. It's because of the way their diaphragm is connected to their backbone. But, in humans, our diaphragms don't have that connection, and we can breathe in whatever pattern we want to or need to."

"So why is that interesting or important?" I say.

And he says, "Humans are really good endurance runners. I know I can outrun a dog, and I think I can maybe outrun a horse on a hot day. So, for some reason, we've evolved this way, and maybe the way we breathe might have something to do with it."

I tell him that's just the opposite of what I've read in my anthropology classes—bipedalism is a bad design that causes problems with knees and backs and feet, and that it only came about as a way to free the hands to make and use tools and weapons.

My brother has a vein that bulges out of his forehead whenever he gets tense or upset, and when I say that bipedalism is a bad design, that vein pops out like a map of the Nile River. He says, "The people who write those things are fat, sweatered geeks who never get up from their desk, and, besides, there's just no evidence to support the tool-use theory—tools don't show up in the archeological record until about two million years after the first bipedal hominids. And another thing, if bipedalism is such a bad design, why can we run farther than just about any other animal?"

"Well, how do you explain it?" I ask.

And he says, "Bipedalism may be an adaptation for endurance running, and maybe our earliest ancestors could run down big game without using any weapons at all. I've found ethnographic accounts of primitive people who were able to do it—the Tarahumara in Mexico could run down deer, the Aborigines in Australia could run down kangaroo, the Goshutes and Papago here in the West are said to have been able to run down pronghorn antelope. I tried it last summer with some antelope in Wyoming, just for an hour or so, and they basically ditched me, but I want to try it again. I could use some help if you want to do it. "

I say, "You want to run down an antelope?"

"I don't know if we can, but I'd like to try it again."

"It seems to make sense, and it also seems impossible," I say. "It would take a lot of work on my part—getting in shape, learning to run long distances, most likely only to fail in the end."

"Failure is not necessarily a bad thing in science," he says, "and, besides, what else have you got going?"

"I was kind of planning to fail in my own way. I thought that was the point."

"Count it as research."

"Yeah, fine," I say, "whatever."

windfall

When I was nineteen, my mother bought an old house for ten thousand dollars and said I could live in it if I cleaned it up and took care of it. It sat in the weeds on a narrow, dead-end alley two blocks from the University of Utah. I was just back in town after wandering around for nearly a year, and maybe she wanted me to go to school, maybe it was a tax write-off, or both. I said sure and moved in—or, rather, I opened the door and set my backpack down on the floor.

The first night I spent in the house, my neighbor from across the alley came over for a visit. He was in his mid-forties, six-foot-two, with greasy, shoulder-length hair combed straight back, glasses that made his eyes look huge, a six-day beard, and a sixteen-ounce Budweiser in each hand. "Bob Kerry," he said, putting a Bud in my left hand and shaking my right. "Welcome to the neighborhood."

"Down on the corner," he said, "you got the two old lesbians. They're nosy as hell and a pure nuisance. They just put up two security lights that shine straight in my bedroom. Then, next door, there's the crazy hag from Tennessee. She drinks Thunderbird all day and screams at her speed-freak son to go out and get a job. I've been here longer than anybody. It's my mom's house, but she lives in San Francisco now, managing a hotel, the one in that film *The Conversation*. You seen it?"

"Yeah," I said, "it's one of my favorites. Harry Caul, a man who makes his living spying on other people, recording their conversations, and yet he's so shy and protective of his own privacy that he wears his raincoat to bed."

"That was a great movie," he said. "Flushed the bitch down the toilet."

"No," I said, "it was all a setup. Actually the two lovers killed the rich husband and flushed him down the toilet."

"Whatever. The ending was awesome, the best ending of any movie I've ever seen, bar none."

"You mean how he completely gutted his house, obsessed with finding the hidden microphone?"

"I mean the way, in the last shot, he's just sitting there playing his saxophone, like he doesn't give a fuck about anything anymore." He said this in a forceful manner, with spit flying from his lips, and then spent a few seconds glaring at me with magnified eyes, his head cocked to one side.

"Yes, exactly," I said, taking a long pull on my beer, waiting for another topic by which to discover and negotiate the terms of our incipient neighborship.

Bob said he used to work in construction and concrete, but that he'd fallen from a ladder and injured his leg and was living on disability, which didn't go very far. He said he made up the difference by "doing jobs for 'The Man.'" He wanted me to know that he had this kind of experience and that I could count on him, no matter what.

"Listen," he said, "I can tell just by looking at you that you're a smart son of a bitch who doesn't know his ass from his elbow. If you need something done, I mean, if you got somebody you want fixed—beaten up or disappeared—you tell me and it's as good as done. You just ask Bob."

"Yeah, O.K.," I said, "but things are going pretty good right now, thanks anyway."

I completely gutted the house. Tore out any walls that weren't holding up the roof, stripping nine layers of paper off the others, ripping up the carpet, breaking the window frames free of paint and opening them for the first time in decades. I kept only the refrigerator and the stove. I slept on a camping pad on the floor with a stray kitten purring on my neck.

Bob would come over every day and drink beer, smoke Pall Malls and watch me work, offering advice. In the beginning, his friend Clarence was staying with him. Clarence was sixty years old and had white hair. He was just "holing up" until he went to prison for killing his wife. I asked him whether he'd been falsely accused, and he said no, that he'd been drunk, which was no excuse. Then I asked him how he did it, and he said, "With a broomstick, 'cause she was a witch." They'd come over with folding lawn chairs in order to sit and drink beer and listen to jazz on my tape player. They were Bob's tapes. He had John Coltrane, Miles Davis and Fats Waller. They'd drink two or three beers and Bob would get up and move around, not dancing, but moving to the music, saying, "You hear that? You hear that man? Awesome." And Clarence would say, "Oh shit, it's just noise. Let me put in some Hank Williams, and we'll hear some real music." It would go on like this through three beers, four beers, then, somewhere around two six-packs, they'd be yelling at each other, making no sense whatsoever, while I carried out lath and plaster and threw it in a pile in the front yard.

Clarence went to the state penitentiary. He wrote me a letter from there saying that I was a good man and that I should try not to make the same mistakes he had, but that, all in all, prison wasn't so bad. He said he thanked God every day he wasn't in for lying or cheating or stealing, as these men had nothing to look forward to but getting beat up and becoming some man's girlfriend.

So Clarence was gone, and the old woman from Tennessee disappeared one day, which left Bob and me and the two lesbians down on the corner. Sometimes they'd stop by in the afternoon when Bob was sleeping and ask me all kinds of questions—"Who was my mom anyway to buy this house for me?" "Why didn't I have a job?" And, "Why did I let that awful Mr. Kerry come over and bother me?" They had visited his house and had seen a sawed-off shotgun standing by the front door. They were "concerned about what the alley was becoming." They were "afraid" they might have to "build a block wall" around their house. They wanted me to do something about "that man," and then they wanted me to paint the outside of my house.

Bob did keep his shotgun by the door, but I thought of it as being like a trophy, something of a conversation starter more than an actual tool. I thought the whole thing about him being a hit man was just his way of trying to impress people. It was hard to believe he had ever killed anyone.

Then, one night, he came over at eleven o'clock, oddly sober and heavily oiled, looking slick in a black shirt and white tie, clean shaven. He was shaking. He said he just wanted to say good-bye because he might not be around for a while. His hand was cold and wet when I shook it.

The next day he was sitting in my living room while I was painting, and he never said a thing about what had happened the night before. But a few months later he was gone for ten days, and I thought maybe he was on the run. It turned out he'd been in the hospital with a broken leg. He'd gone over to the Top Stop at midnight for a quart of beer and was hit by a drunk driver coming back across Fifth East. He had a cast from his crotch to his ankle. I said, "I'm sorry man," and he said, "No way, it's the best thing that could have happened. Sure, it hurt like a motherfucker, but then they shot me up and I was flying. Now I'm going to sue the son of a bitch for everything he has. My lawyer says it will be in the hundreds of thousands, maybe a million. I'm rich!"

The accident changed his life. He decided to go to school and get a degree in technical drawing. He took math and wrote some papers, and he'd come over with his homework and tests to show me how well he was doing. He was proud of himself. He even had a girlfriend for a while—a woman his age who was studying to be an accountant. But she turned out to be trouble. Bob had a party one night for her and her friends. It was a wild party that I would have been invited to, but I was out of town. I went over to his house after I got home, and the place was torn apart. There were pills and all kinds of pharmaceuticals on the kitchen table. There were syringes and a vial of liquid opium. There was a hole, two feet in diameter, blown through the ceiling in his living room. He said that one of the guests had gotten paranoid about the police and had used the shotgun to make "an escape route" through the roof.

Bob put away the sawed-off shotgun, and I never saw the girlfriend again. He left that kind of life behind. His lawyer was working on the lawsuit, and, as far as Bob knew, he was going to be rich. He was going to be a new man. When not in school or studying, he spent his time making a list of what he was going to buy with all the money: two Harley Davidsons (an Electroglide and a Sportster) and a pickup truck to haul them around; a new four-way stereo system with a 500-watt Kenwood amplifier and six-foot-high JBL speakers; and an elaborate, hand-carved bar for entertaining friends. He carried the list of these things in his shirt pocket so he could add and subtract continually, day by day, month by month.

And then there were the plans for his new home. He was going to rebuild his house, which was a small brick box, by first raising it fifteen feet off the ground on steel I beams. Then he was going to take off his roof and add another three floors on top, pagoda-style. He had it drawn out in all dimensions and angles—a sixty-foot-tall pagoda with dragons and flames flaring out from sloping gables. Every detail was drafted down to the framing and nailing schedules.

In one way, the promise of money seemed like a disease, a mental illness, where Bob began believing that these dreams had already materialized. But, in another way, he wasn't dreaming. He kept his hair cut, he changed his clothes, he stopped using so much cologne— he even stopped coming over and spending the day. He was a new man because he had all this stuff . . . even though he didn't actually have any of it.

The lawsuit dragged on and on. One year. Two years. In the end, he got very little. Maybe a few thousand dollars. The lawyer's bill was quite high, and I suppose the judge decided that Bob's life hadn't really been damaged so much after all. Before the accident, he'd been a bum; after the accident, he'd earned a degree in technical drawing and had become something better than a bum. But I'm guessing at this point. He never really told me what happened. He was just too depressed to talk about it. He stayed inside his house, watching television and drinking beer.

Then one day he was gone. He left me a note saying he went to San Francisco to live with his mother and didn't know when he'd be back. Not long after that, I left town to go to school out-of-state, and I've never heard from him since. I picture him sitting in the basement of the Jack-Tar Hotel, the one in *The Conversation*, with a lousy mattress and his sawed-off shotgun, listening to Miles and waiting to be called upstairs by The Man for a job, disposing of the evidence by flushing it down the toilet.

1984

In the summer my brother and I go to Wyoming to try to run down an antelope. The idea is not to run faster than the antelope—only cheetahs can run faster than pronghorn antelope—but to run longer and farther in the heat of the day. My brother thinks it will take about two hours and then the antelope will overheat and collapse.

We drive off the interstate and down a dirt road for a few miles and it's a wide and open high desert of sagebrush, dry as a bone, mountains in every direction. There are antelope everywhere—in pairs, in clusters, in families, alone.

We stop the car and start running after three—a buck and two does. They run very quickly, but for short distances, and then stop and stare at us until we catch up. Then they take off again. Sometimes they run a quarter of a mile, sometimes a half mile.

My brother is a much better runner than me, and I'm way behind him, looking out for sagebrush and rattlesnakes and cactus, tired but laughing. It's a lot more fun than running down the street or even up in the mountains. I keep my brother in sight, and, although I sometimes lose the antelope, I can tell they're running in a broad arc, clockwise, and so I aim to cut them off. I catch up with them, even ahead of my brother, and they stand there and let me get within fifty yards.

Pronghorn antelope have big black eyes—eyes the size you'd see on a horse. The three antelope look at me like they know exactly what we're proposing, and they're not in the least bit worried. They look at me, and I stare back, and this goes on for maybe a couple of minutes—I don't know, I can't say, because something happens. It's like being hypnotized or being abducted by aliens who take me to a planet where things happen that I can't remember. Then, suddenly, the three antelope break the spell and fly off, running. I turn and see my brother coming up, all red and sweating.

We chase them over a little hill, and on the other side the three have become eight, and they're a long way off, so it's impossible to tell which three we began chasing. We follow them for five or ten minutes and then they split into three groups, each going in a different direction. We can't tell which group has even one of the antelope we started chasing, they all look so much alike, especially from a distance. We choose two does and follow them, and they run over another hill. On the other side, all of a sudden, there are twenty of them, running as a herd.

Following this herd is like following a school of fish. They blend and flow and change positions. There are no individuals, but this mass that moves across the desert like a pool of mercury on a glass table. Then they split again, bursting into five pieces, and it's just too confusing; we can't tell whether we're chasing animals that have run for two minutes or twenty minutes or two hours.

I catch up with my brother, and he says, "Man, did you see them run? They just zoom and they're gone." I ask him how we're going to get around how they group and split like that, and he says, "I don't know, I've been thinking about it and I don't know."

"What do you think we should do?" I ask.

"I think we should try it again. Let's find some more."

And so we do. We chase antelope off and on for two days, but, basically, they just ditch us every time.

come to stay

I remember sitting on my front steps in the morning waiting for her to ride up the hill on her bicycle. It was in spring, late April, and it had been raining, steam coming up off the street and sidewalks. I was waiting on the steps and realized that I was in love with her and that everything was going to be different now. She would ride up and set her bike down on the grass and we would go inside and she would live there with me for a long time, maybe forever. I knew it. I saw the whole thing coming. The only thing missing was the ending.

My house had no furniture other than two chairs and a table. I made some coffee and moved the table over by the window so she could sit in the sun. She was a modern dancer, small and thin, wearing a white cotton blouse, no bra, shorts and sandals, and sweating a bit from the ride. Her skin was dark-tanned already so early, lovely legs but with lots of scars on the knees and shins, and her feet were like little creatures unto themselves, beautiful and frightening. They had the structure of the Golden Gate Bridge—a high, sinewy arch with built-in springs and pulleys, and long toes stretching out for purchase.

I'd seen her dance the night before in front of a small audience downtown. I disliked most modern dance, but she had a unique style, one wrapped around the idea that she really weighed nothing at all, and that her body was only there to tell a story. I asked her if she liked my house, and she said she liked the view. She asked me what I thought about her concert, and I said I thought it was funny. She said, "Funny? Only funny?"

"Funny and beautiful," I said.

And she said, "That's better."

Up until this time I had been living alone and was not unhappy. I had a house, a dog, a car. No job. I had money from the National Endowment for the Arts to produce a radio story about chasing antelope, which only required, as far as I could tell, a wholehearted effort to live as much like a primitive as possible. It was a problem I was working on by myself. My plan was to live simply and to stay outside and cover as much ground as possible.

But there she was, come to stay.

She asked me why I had only one fork in the kitchen. I said it was all I needed, then asked how many she had in her kitchen.

"Eight," she said, "and at least ten spoons, and I have some glasses, different kinds, even wine glasses. I like to have friends over. I like to cook and have friends over to eat. Don't you have any friends?"

"Yeah, I have a friend, but he doesn't have any hands," I said, looking over at my dog.

"You know," she said, "I've been dreaming about you. I think I'm in love with you."

I went downstairs and brought up the pieces of a wooden bed frame that had been left there by a previous tenant. I had the mattress and everything, and I asked where she would like to have it. She said, "I like to sit in bed in the morning and drink coffee." So I moved the table and put the bed there in the sunlight.

1987

Last night a thunderclap woke me from my sleep. This morning there's new snow on the mountains, six to ten inches at ten thousand feet. It will be gone, melt and transpire, before the sun sets. The first storm of the season, the smell of the furnace burning the summer's dust.

My brother has gone away to get a Ph.D. at a big university back east. The campus is flat and surrounded by trees, and he no longer thinks about chasing antelope. He studies lizards now.

I stay in Salt Lake. I try to leave, but it seems like I have a rubber band attached. What is it that pulls me back? No place is more beautiful than the Salt Lake Valley. Other places are just as beautiful, but when it comes down to a contest this place wins. Beauty is something to be studied over a long period of time, and there needs to be some point of reference—these clouds over these mountains, compared to what? The city itself has the most admirable quality of a ghost town, dry as a bone and empty as a rattle. People are leaving in droves for a better life on the Coast. I, however, wait for the coast to come to me. I get up in the foothills above my house, look out across the entire valley and see it covered by water, as it was only ten thousand years ago. I extend my arm and wave my hand across the inland sea and think, "Someday my son, all of this will be yours."

I have a plan: get in shape and live like a primitive. I've read a lot about "primitive" cultures. I use the term primitive in the sense that it means original or primary. I see culture as being the ability to make something out of nothing, a kind of magic. It started with a joke—

that the first human act was somebody trying to make somebody else laugh. Apes and dogs and other animals have a sense of humor, but only human beings can tell a joke. These are my conclusions, completely unsupported by the literature.

Human beings began as hunters and gatherers, and stayed hunters and gatherers for two million years, or ninety-nine percent of our history. Our bodies and minds have evolved out of this cultural environment. So, I've decided that in order to live as a "natural" human being, I need to try live like a hunter and gatherer. Which is impossible. Even if I were to wake up naked and alone in the wilderness, I would still wake up thinking and making sense of myself and the world around me in modern English, and there's no way I can get away from that.

I try to get in shape by running in the mountains and skiing cross-country. I smoke marijuana and eat LSD and mushrooms and try to get lost to the point where I am deeply humbled and almost die trying to make it back. This is my training. And I am not alone. There are many others in the mountains and deserts doing the same thing. None, however, have run down an antelope.

trout stream families

The sun is going down and three families are camped beside a trout stream in southern Utah. The women are talking to each other by the picnic table, the men are watching the children play in the water. Two of the women are sisters. One has just had an affair with a man in Los Angeles. On the phone she swore to her sister that she would tell her husband and insist on a divorce. But now she's thinking she will not say anything, ever, about the affair, and maybe wait a while on the divorce. Her sister is swaying back and forth with a baby in her arms. This morning, the baby stuck her right hand in a cup of hot coffee and cried for hours. Now she's asleep, but her fingers have big, balloon-like blisters that will break and heal slowly, leaving long white scars. The third woman is two days pregnant and thinking about taking a nap.

Of the men, one is trying to decide when would be the best time to drive into town and call his broker; one is thinking about running up the mountain to smoke a joint and watch the sun go down; the other is looking at the water, wondering if the fish might like a grasshopper.

The children are playing and fighting over a toy sailboat in the water. The three-year-old boy is soaking wet and nearly out of his mind with possibilities. The five-year-old girl is standing on the bank, making up rules and shouting out orders and dropping lettuce and cheese from her sandwich.

There are little birds in the trees, and big birds on the rock walls of the canyon—red rock walls in the shadow of the afternoon sun. A dirt road comes around and down and crosses over the stream, and in the pool below the road a pale snake slides silently into the water and swims to the other side, holding something rather large in its mouth.

There are three cars, all white, and there's an Indian, or rather the ghost of an Indian who lived and died in this spot, sitting cross-legged on the hood of a station wagon.

This is the beginning of a story. The story is about how the husband realizes his wife has been unfaithful, and it's about how the Indian died, and what the snake had in its mouth, and how the two-day-old life inside the mother grows, and is born, and becomes a beautiful young woman who paints the poems of Rilke on the desert blacktop highway.

The sun is going down and three families are camped beside a trout stream in southern Utah.

1990

I found an ethnography, dated 1935, on the Tarahumara, one of the tribes my brother said can run down big game.

> *The Tarahumara keep the deer constantly on the move. Only occasionally does he get a glimpse of his quarry, but follows it unerringly through his own canny ability to read the tracks. The Indian chases the deer until the creature falls from exhaustion, often with its hooves completely worn away. It is then throttled by the man or killed by the dogs.*
>
> W. C. Bennett and R. M. Zingg, *The Tarahumara: An Indian Tribe of Northern Mexico* (Chicago: University of Chicago Press, 1935), p. 113.

But then this was written by a couple of anthropologists who didn't actually go out and hunt with the Indians, so there's no way to know whether this is actually true. There's no doubt, though, that the Tarahumara are crazy about running. Another ethnography (Bernard Fontana's 1989 *The Tarahumara*) describes races where a group of men from a village eat peyote and smear themselves with white grease and run as a team, tossing a leather ball the size of a hackeysack down a trail with their toes. They run for three days, close to three hundred miles, and the winning team gets to sleep with all the available women in the local village.

This is the way I want to live.

the friendly man

There are many bad ways to wake up; surely one of the worst is by looking into the floodlight from a police car. I was in a field, some farmer's field, next to a power plant just outside Lawrence, Kansas. I was sleeping there next to my car before driving into Kansas City, Missouri, in the morning. The policemen saw my car from the road and pulled up right in front of it. When I woke up, one policeman was in the front seat—I guess looking for drugs—and the other was forty feet away in the hay field. I don't know why he was out there unless he had his gun pulled, covering his partner. He said I scared him when I awoke and sat up so suddenly. He could have shot me dead.

They wanted to know what I was doing sleeping in the field. I told them that I didn't like motels, which was only partly true, so I told them that I was born there, in Lawrence, but that I didn't live there anymore, which was completely true but somehow didn't achieve the level of meaning I hoped it would. They asked me what I was going to do in Kansas City, and I said that I was going to interview the mayor at 11:00 A.M.

Then I told them that I was a producer for a radio program. I told them the name of the program and the name of the host, and they'd heard of him. You'd also know who he is if I were to say his name; instead, I have decided to call him the Friendly Man, because that is his persona. Every weekday morning the Friendly Man has a five-minute feed on one of the radio networks, and twelve million people listen. His stories are upbeat and positive; their general theme is people taking responsibility for their lives, their community, their country. The Friendly Man always has good news and the good news is always that America just keeps getting better and better. Both policemen said that they had heard the program and that they liked the Friendly Man, and so they decided they liked me as well. They said it was okay to sleep in the field and they were sorry to have bothered me.

Some people are surprised to hear that the Friendly Man doesn't actually produce the stories he tells. It's not that he doesn't want to write his stories, not that he can't, it's just that he's really busy now being the Friendly Man—making appearances and doing TV—and he shouldn't be expected to come up with all his own material.

So the way it works is this: The Friendly Man is in New York and his executive producers are in San Francisco, and the researchers are all over the place looking for story ideas through computer searches. When a researcher finds a story, he calls the people mentioned in it and then writes out a synopsis, which is sent to the Friendly Man for approval. Once approved, the story gets assigned to a producer—someone out in the world, like me—who conducts the same interviews all over again, on tape this time, and then edits the tape and writes a script, two and a half minutes long, which is reviewed by the executive producers in San Francisco and sent to the Friendly Man in New York City so he can read it on the air.

The first story I produced for the Friendly Man was about some people in Tucson, Arizona, who were helping to make America a better place by sending juvenile delinquents to a "teen court" where they would be sentenced by a jury of other juvenile delinquents. I called an audio engineer in Tucson, and had him go to the locations and hold up a microphone to the subjects while I talked to them on the phone. Then he sent me the tape, which I edited, and I wrote the script without ever meeting the people I was writing about or the person I was writing for. Basically, all I did was just fill in the researcher's synopsis with quotes, which was all I was supposed to do. When I made a suggestion for changing the story, a change I thought would make it better, the executive producer said she would try not to get upset with me because this was my first story and maybe I didn't understand my role: the story had been approved as written in the synopsis; there were to be no changes, no additional narratives, or discoveries. I was but the producer/writer. For me to suggest a change was like suggesting that everyone else had made a mistake. I apologized and did the story as ordered.

After this first story I asked the executive producer if I could go on the road, drive around and collect interviews, actually meet the people and see what they were doing. She gave me four stories, set in four different cities, which would require driving 3,000 miles. They would pay the mileage but would give nothing up front. The food and lodging were to be my expenses, and so I was sleeping out. It was the first week of July, and so warm at night you could sleep on the grass without a bag or a blanket.

At 11:00 on the morning after the incident with the police, I was standing in the mayor's office on the top floor of the Kansas City Missouri Municipal Building. It was a tall building, built on top of the highest hill in the area, so looking out the window I could see most of the city, buildings and railroad tracks and the Missouri River making a big oxbow right through town.

We sat in tall chairs at a long conference table. Mayor Emanuel Cleaver, a black mayor in a black town, was also a Methodist minister. I'd come to ask him about his midnight basketball program, which was designed to reduce the crime rate by keeping juveniles off the street. But the crime rate hadn't gone down, except for the time that the kids were actually playing basketball. The mayor's opponents were saying that the program was pork, that the $100,000 a year could be better spent elsewhere. But the mayor was passionate about the value of teaching kids to play basketball. He said that team sports teach kids the best values: they learn to cooperate and play by the rules, they learn to love the game, and through the love of the game they learn to love themselves and each other. He said that a few of the kids had gone to college on basketball scholarships, and this gave hope to everybody in the community, a community where hope was like a foreign language. "You go to the games," he said, "it's mothers, fathers, sisters and brothers—you'll see the whole community there."

I went over to the east side, the poor side of town, where the games were going on in a community center. The place was packed and the games were good, with little eight- and nine-year-old boys passing the ball and making plays and running hard the whole game. I interviewed coaches, kids and parents, and it seemed that things really were getting better and better in America. But then, just before I left, somebody took my three rechargeable batteries and the audio tape with the mayor's interview on it out of my bag and out of the building. And they were gone. The batteries were worth $250 and could be replaced, but the interview with the mayor was lost for good.

I walked around the neighborhood for a while, trying to figure out what to do. The next day was a Saturday, and I doubted the mayor would be at his office, which would mean that I would have to wait till Monday, but I had appointments for interviews Monday morning for another story in St. Louis, 250 miles to the east. And then there was the fact that I had been robbed while doing a story about a program that reduces juvenile crime. The story as it was written by the researcher in the synopsis was all about how black people were improving their lives and making things better by playing basketball, but the reality of the situation, at least the way I saw it, was that these people were poor, that they'd been poor for a long time and that they were probably going to stay poor for a long time. So I called the executive producer and left her a message saying that maybe she should consider scrapping the basketball story, and that I was going on to St. Louis and would call her from there.

The story in St. Louis was also about poor black people, only in St. Louis it was old poor black people who lived in a nursing home and had started their own private economy wherein they would get paid for helping each other out—by washing clothes, or cooking meals, or even reading books and stories out loud at bedtime. But they didn't get paid in real money; they got paid in what they called "time dollars," which could be exchanged only between themselves or cashed in at a special community store for food, clothing and other necessary items. The old people liked the time dollar program; they were much happier than before they had the time dollar program. This is what the researcher had written in the synopsis, and this is how things seemed for most of the morning I was there doing interviews.

My first interview was with the upper-middle-class white woman who'd set everything up. She worked for a large charitable organization as a local manager of its programs, such as the time dollar store in the old folks' home. She'd written a brochure explaining the program, and it was nicely produced. She told me that the program had won an award. Everything seemed fine, but the woman was very nervous and I couldn't tell if it was because she was just nervous being interviewed, or if she was nervous being surrounded by poor black people. I talked to her for a while, and then she introduced me to some women who actually participated in the time dollar program. They told me that they do things like call up old people around town and ask them if they feel okay, or they clean and dry a neighbor's clothes before he goes into the hospital in the morning, or they cook for someone who has bad asthma. And then they can use the time dollars to buy stuff they need. They were friendly ladies, and it was just like it said in the synopsis: neighbors helping neighbors and getting paid to do it.

So I asked them if we could go over and see the store where they bought everything. They sort of hemmed and hawed about it and said there was a key and they'd have to get it. Then they started talking about grandchildren and arthritis and the weather in Mississippi. I asked again about the store, and they said it was a couple of blocks away and it was raining. At this point I began to worry, because the time-dollar store was in the synopsis and there had to be some tape of it in the story, and so I explained my predicament and begged them to take me there.

We borrowed some umbrellas and walked over to the building

that housed the store. It was a one-story warehouse, brick and concrete with a few windows. We went down a hallway that separated two large rooms, each packed with desks and stacks of paper, stacks of folders, desks fans, lots of desk lights, people typing on real typewriters and adding machines. It was all very suspicious.

Down at the far, dark end of the hall was a large metal cabinet with two full-length doors locked with a padlock. One of the ladies opened the lock and inside were four shelves: the top held bottles of fabric softener, the next was full of baby wipes, another had some paper plates and plastic silverware, and the bottom had bathroom deodorizer. That was it. That was the store. I had imagined something between a 7-Eleven and a thrift store, and I didn't understand. I didn't understand how any of this was working. The story had disintegrated into baby wipes and picnic forks.

I thanked the ladies and left the building and called the executive producer in San Francisco. I didn't want to tell her about the baby wipes and the fabric softener; there was no use in saying that the whole story was a sham. But I did want to ask her if it would be okay if I left the store out of the story, that maybe the story should be that these people just like to help each other and that the time dollar thing wasn't so important. But she never let me get to it. She was upset, very upset, about the message I had left on her machine Friday night. She said it had ruined her whole weekend. She was distraught and nearly hysterical, saying everyone on her staff was distraught and nearly hysterical, and it was my fault—my fault to have taken my eyes off my equipment, my fault to have been robbed, my fault to have left town without completing the story assignment. She said that I had led her to believe that I was a professional, but that no professional would behave in such a manner. She said this twice, the subtext being that the Friendly Man can only use professional producers, and therefore I was fired—unless, maybe, I went back to Kansas City to reinterview the mayor. My job was to do what I was told, just as their job was to do what they were told, because the audience, the twelve million listeners, had something they wanted to be told: that America is a good place with decent people, never mind the screaming coming from the basement.

So I got in my car and drove two hundred and fifty miles west to Kansas City. I went back because I didn't want to be fired by the Friendly Man. I had been fired by other, less well-known "friendly men," and it was always like being branded, scorned as the one who ran. I was tired of that, tired of being broke and not having any work. My wife, my family—they were tired of it too. I decided that I wanted to be a professional, that I wanted to be a team player, that I wanted to take responsibility for my life, my community and my country, and get ahead and go someplace with my career and be happy.

I drove back to Kansas City and got in late at night. I drove past the big buildings downtown, through the streets lit yellow and vacant. I drove through the poor neighborhoods and along the parkways, past fountains and parks, and I drove by my grandmother's house and down to the Country Club Plaza where I slept without a bag or a blanket on the lawn, on the long esplanade in front of the Nelson Art Museum. If I was to be bothered by the police, I would tell them that I was a radio producer working for the Friendly Man and that I had a meeting with the mayor in the morning.

1991

The larger objects of the feral chase are deer, antelope, and mountain sheep, to which the puma, jaguar, and two or three other carnivores might be added. The chase is conducted by no more than five men who scatter at the sight of the quarry in such a manner as to partially surround it; when it takes flight one after the other strives to show himself above the shrubbery or dunes in order to break its line of flight into a series of zigzags; and whether successful in this effort or not they keep approximate pace with it until it tires, then gradually surround it and finally rush in to either seize it in their hands or cripple it with clubs — though the latter procedure is deemed undignified, if not wrong and hardly less disreputable than complete failure. The dissection is merely a ravenous rending of skin and flesh, primarily with the teeth, and partly with some improvised device such as a horn or tooth of the victim itself. Commonly the entire animal is gulped at a single sitting in which the zeal of the devotee and the frenzy of the carnivore blend. The leg bones are split for the marrow, the horns are retained as talismann-trophies, while the skin is stretched and kept for bedding or robe or kilt.

William McGhee, *Report to the Smithsonian Institution on the Seri Indians of Mexico*, 1895

My brother has spent five years trying to get a Ph.D., and it seems like the whole thing is killing him. He's developed a heart condition called a ventricular fribrulation, which means that the upper and lower chambers beat out of sync with each other and his blood doesn't circulate properly. It only happens for short periods, and only when he's really tired or extremely tense and nervous, like when he runs too far, or right before he has to defend his dissertation. He feels suddenly woozy and has to sit down, and sometimes he passes out. So, I've written a letter to his adviser and have come to Ann Arbor to hand deliver it:

Dear Dr. Renzer,

I assume that you are aware of my brother's heart condition and probably even believe you understand the pathology involved. Let me be perfectly clear: if my brother dies while under your supervision you can kiss your own sweet ass good-bye.

Scott Carrier

I drive into town late Sunday night and the doors to the biology building are locked. I've been here a couple of times before and I sort of remember where my brother's lab is located, so I take a guess and throw a rock at a window, and it's his and he's there.

In his lab, on a table, is a three-foot-long monitor lizard lying perfectly still except for an occasional blink of an eye. Two tiny wires are dangling out of its rib cage. He has anesthetized it and implanted electrodes into its intercostal muscles, or the muscles along the rib cage.

He puts the lizard in its box and takes me to the basement where he has built a long runway of plywood and two-by-fours. He has another big lizard down there, and he takes it out of the cage and holds it and puts it on his shoulders, and it jumps through three feet of air and lands on the wall and sticks to the cinder block like Spider-man. He yanks it off the wall and puts it at one end of the runway.

"Watch how its backbone moves when it runs," he says.

Then he touches its tail and it blasts off down the track. Its backbone waves like a plucked guitar string.

"I thought that lizards probably can't breathe when they run," he says. "I thought the way they bend like that would make it impossible."

"And do they breathe when they run?"

"No, it looks like they can't run and breathe at the same time."

"So why has it taken you so long? Why have you been doing this for five years?"

He explains that he's upset some people, some "dinosaur people," and that he's had to go back and do all his experiments all over again. I ask him why the dinosaur people are upset, and he tells me that dinosaurs were lizards but that they could run like mammals, bending their backs vertically instead of horizontally, which, he believed, was the next step in the evolution of breathing. It was a good theory, but so new as to be suspect.

I tell him I'm going to Mexico to run down a deer with the Tarahumara. I tell him he should come, but he says there's no way he can go, no way he can leave his work. He doesn't even seem interested, and I drive out of town without delivering the letter and thinking, "Now it's just me. Now I'm in this alone."

the test

I was hired to interview men and women in the state of Utah who receive Medicaid support for treatment of mental illnesses generally diagnosed as schizophrenia; my work was to be part of a larger study to test the effectiveness of Medicaid payments. I was told that they needed someone willing to drive around the state, through the small towns, searching out individuals who were often transient and prone to hiding. I had just quit my steady job, my professional job as a radio reporter, after realizing that what I wanted more than anything was to put my boss on the floor, stand on his throat and watch him gag. Then my wife moved out, took the kids and everything. She said, "I've thought about it, and I really think it's the best thing for me at this time in my life." So I accepted the job interviewing schizophrenics. I took it because it was offered to me and because it was all there seemed to be.

I was trained to administer the test. There were about a hundred questions pertaining to anxiety, anger, depression, paranoia, delusions, hallucinations and out-of-body experiences. I was to listen to each answer and then assign a score between one and seven, with one being the best, most healthy score indicating that the client had not been afflicted in the previous week. A two or three meant that, yes, some problems had arisen but they were not long lasting: "Yes, I thought I wanted to hit him, but then I calmed down, and now I don't want to hit him anymore." A four or a five indicated some problems and some difficulty dealing with them or making them go away: "The television talks to me, even when it's turned off. I know these are hallucinations but I can't make them stop." A six or a seven were to be given only in cases where the person was acting out hallucinations, trying to commit suicide, or doing harm to themselves or others. The test took about an hour to complete. The clients were paid five dollars and I was paid thirty, plus gas and mileage.

The client is twenty-three years old and appears perplexed and withdrawn. She says she hears voices telling her she is going to be burned alive. She sits in a chair, mumbling to herself and not responding to any questions; then she gets up, shouting, and starts running around the kitchen and living room like an excited puppy. Her mother tries to catch her but can't, so she just follows her around saying, "Everything will be all right, everything is going to be fine."

The man is at least eighty years old and lives in a nursing home in central Utah. He has no muscle control, no hair, and has to be tied into a wheel chair or he will slide out onto the floor. He answers every question by saying, "I can't remember."

"Have you had trouble making everyday decisions?"

"I can't remember."

"Have you had trouble concentrating?"

"I can't remember."

"Have you felt as if you were outside of your own body, or as if a part of your body does not belong to you? Have you felt like you were floating, like you were in a dream? Have things seemed unreal?"

"I can't remember."

The client stopped being a prostitute when she was in a restaurant in Salt Lake across from Temple Square and realized that she was surrounded by zombies, the living dead, dried-out corpses eating with forks and spoons that held nothing but air. She walked to the hospital and turned herself in.

Last year she was in the hospital again and thought the staff was taking little boys out back and killing them and leaving their bodies behind the building. She could smell the bodies decaying behind the Dumpster.

Her boyfriend has left to go to Mexico for a vacation.

I drive around all day, trying to find a Navajo man. He lives very close to the Four Corners, where Utah, Colorado, New Mexico and Arizona meet. It's all dirt roads, a house every five miles or so, no addresses, no phones. I stop at every house, but either nobody's home or nobody will answer. I flag down every car that passes and ask directions, and the people offer complicated instructions that I try to follow, sometimes driving for twenty or thirty miles. But it's always the wrong place, or nobody's home or there just isn't a house there at all.

Eventually I find the man, or at least I think he's the man. I'm a third of the way through the test before I realize he's not the right guy:

"When was your last visit to a mental health clinic?"

"I don't go to the clinic."

"When did you last see a doctor?"

"I don't have a doctor."

"Do you blame yourself for anything you have done or not done?"

"No."

"Have you felt more self-confident than usual?"

"No."

"Have you heard voices or other things that weren't there or that other people couldn't hear or seen things that were not there?"

And he says, "I think you want to talk to my son."

I ask him what his son's name is, and he says, "Same as mine."

I come back the next morning and interview the son in the kitchen. They make coffee for me on a propane camp stove, because the house has no electricity. The son is nineteen years old, tall, healthy, says he used to run cross-country in high school. He seems to be fine, but midway through the test he fixes his eyes on mine, staring straight into my head like he's trying to pull me in and trap me. I try to look back, to look just as deeply into his mind, but it's like looking into a black hole.

He says he hears voices, satanic voices, and that he worries a lot about his shoes, that they're not the right kind, not the kind he sees on MTV. I can't tell if he's sick or if he's just trying to torture me, and

I drive away thinking I don't know anything about this disease, that I know even less than when I started. I spent two days driving around and made thirty bucks. And I feel really, really tired.

The client is a middle-aged woman who wrings her hands continually through the interview. Her son was run over by a semi when he was six and he lost a leg. Her husband was killed in a coal-mining accident shortly after they were divorced. Her twin sister's husband shot his brother and his wife (six times each with a shotgun) over a land dispute. She worries about her children, about being able to take care of them. She is afraid the housing authorities want to hurt her. She thinks about eating the pills again.

The people I interview all seem to have thin souls, like ghosts and demons have invaded their hearts. A person's soul should be like an ocean, but a schizophrenic's soul is like a pool of rain in a parking lot. They suffer, and they are completely alone in their suffering—no family, no friends, not even a self. And there is nothing I can do, nothing anyone can do, to bring them back.

When she pulled out all her hair . . .

When his mother ran over his head in the driveway . . .

When he fought with Satan and broke doors and windows and put his father in the hospital . . .

When she saw the shirts and underwear on the clothesline jump up and dance . . .

When he stopped talking . . .

When he stopped sleeping . . .

When he never stopped sleeping . . .

When he saw his dead mother every night walking around the cemetery in her wedding gown . . .

Today, halfway through an interview with a man in Tooele he says, "I have a crystal in my pouch, do you want to see it?" I say O.K., and he takes it out, a normal crystal, the size of a large paper clip, and he says,

"I can look through this, and it will tell me whether you are a good person or a bad person. What do you want me to do? Do you want me to look through it or not?" My first thought is that I should say, "Do you want to go on with the interview? Maybe when we are done you can look through the crystal." But then I realize that he's really asking me to take *his* test. So, I say "O.K., go ahead," and he puts the crystal up to his eye and turns it clockwise and counterclockwise, back and forth, squinting, looking me up and down. He says, "I can't tell for sure. I'm going to have to read your mind. Here, take my hand." He holds out his right hand with the crystal resting in the palm. I take his hand, and he puts his left hand over mine and squeezes tight and shakes it and goes into a small spasm. Then he lets me go and sort of sits back like he is exhausted. He asks me if I felt anything, and I say, "Maybe a little." And he says, "I sent you a message. I put it in your mind. I told you what is wrong with me."

I'm not supposed to figure out what is wrong with these people. I'm just supposed to ask the questions and score the answers from one to seven. This is partly because I am not a doctor and might get something going that I wouldn't know how to contain, but it's mainly because my supervisors want clean data. They want all the people asking the questions to be doing it the same way. I'm not supposed to get emotional. I'm not supposed to let the client get emotional. The therapy part of the county mental health system is in another department. I wouldn't even know what number to call, and I've been told, more than once, not to worry about it.

I should never have let him take his crystal out of his pouch.

The house is dark as all the windows have heavy curtains pulled nearly shut. The curtains over the big picture window in the living room are open just a bit, and the light cuts through like a laser beam and hits the red shag carpet, throwing up small dust particles and cigarette ash. Two feet away from the light, near the television, a slice of pizza is lying upside down in the carpet. I'm interviewing the woman, a mother, and her teenage daughter is on the phone talking to her boyfriend, or rather a series of boyfriends who call and call, and all of them want her to go out right now but her mother won't let her. She is trying to answer my questions, trying to concentrate and be polite, but she is mainly listening to what her daughter is saying on the phone and will suddenly switch from saying, "No, no, I've been feeling fine. I haven't had a relapse in months" to screaming out, "Is that John? I told you never to talk to him again." Or, "Who is it? Is it a boy? You can't go out. Tell him he has to come over here."

I can't stop looking at the slice of pizza on the carpet. I keep looking at it because it's the only clue that the woman is sick. I mean, she has a teenage daughter and a dirty house and maybe she shouldn't try to wear makeup to bed, but these are not necessarily symptoms of schizophrenia. She seems to be okay until I get to the question, "Have you been worrying a lot?" And she says, yes, she has, she's been worrying that the elders of the church, the Mormon Church, will take her daughter away from her. I ask her why, and she says because she stopped taking her medication. She says that the only reason she takes it is because she told her bishop that she was visited by the Archangel Gabriel and that she'd had sex with him. And then she'd also been visited by the Archangel Michael, and she'd had sex with both of them at once, and they'd ravished her almost every night since. So her bishop made her go to a doctor, and the doctor gave her some pills, and she took the pills, and the angels stopped coming. The bishop and the elders had told her that if she had sex with any more angels they'd take her daughter away.

So I ask her again why she stopped taking the pills and she says, "I'm lonely. I miss them. I want them to come back."

Today, in a restaurant, eating lunch between interviews, I decided to take the test. I answered the questions and scored myself appropriately, and, at some point, I realized I wasn't doing so well. I decided not to add up the points, because then I'd be left with a score and I'd never forget it. If I were to write a report on myself, it would sound something like this: The client is thirty-six years old and lives alone since his wife left him three weeks ago. She took the kids and all the kitchenware except for a large knife and a bowl and a coffee cup. The client admits her leaving may have had something to do with the fact that, without warning, he completely gutted the house. Tore out all the walls and ceilings, all the lath and plaster, right down to the studs. He says he did this in order to live like a primitive. When asked if it was successful, he says, "It was a step in the right direction."

The client is a thirty-six-year-old male who lives alone since his wife and children left him over two months ago. He says there's a darkness that separates him from other people, a heavy darkness, like looking at a person from the bottom of a well. He believes that if he could say the right words, then the darkness would go away. He says he sometimes knows the right words but can't say them. Other times he can't even think of what words to say. He has a very flat affect, speaks only when he is forced to reply, and these words he mumbles almost incoherently. His house has no electricity, he has yet to clean up the lath and plaster debris on the floor, and the window frames have no glass in them. He says, "I feel like I'm living on a meteorite."

The client is thirty-six years old and lives alone since his wife and children left him three months ago. Last week he went fishing in the San Juan Mountains and now believes that there is no better fisherman than himself. He says, "I can't tell you about it, because talking about fishing is silly. All I can say is I walk around in the water, and I know the instant the fish will jump for the fly. I cut open their stomachs and squeeze out the bugs in my hand, study what they eat, how it all gets digested, even the exoskeleton and wings." He says he was sick before, but now he's okay, and that it was the fly rod, just holding the rod in his hand, that cured him. His house is clean, the electricity is on, the walls have been Sheetrocked and painted white.

He says, "I'll have to ask her, beg her, and maybe she'll come back."

1992

In the beginning, God inhaled and created all of life. This is the Hindu creation myth. They have the same word for breath and spirit, as did the ancient Greeks. Over the years, I've realized that my brother is basically writing his own creation myth, although it's couched in evolutionary terms, since he's a vertebrate morphologist and studies the evolution of breathing. His basic premise is that the form and function of an animal, its morphology, will develop around its pulmonary system. All his tests and experiments with lizards, fish, birds and dogs rest on the underlying theory that the lungs and the pulmonary system always change and evolve toward increasing stamina and endurance; that is, the better the animal moves, the better it can find food and avoid becoming food for others. Always, the changes are driven by the need for more breath, and, to be metaphysical, more spirit or soul.

I used to think that if we could run down an antelope it would prove my brother's theory of human evolution, which he called the running hypothesis. It's different from the two dominant theories in anthropology—the hunting hypothesis and the gathering hypothesis—both of which seem inadequate to me. The hunting hypothesis says that we separated from the apes when we became bipedal in order to free the hands to make and use tools and weapons for hunting. But tools, at least stone tools, don't show up in the archeological record until about two million years after the advent of bipedalism. The gathering hypothesis says that we stood upright in order to carry things around, things like extra food, supplies and babies. But the problem here is that this is just totally uninspiring. I carry things every day, all day. I work as a carpenter's helper or as a grip on film productions, and there's nothing in carrying things around that makes me feel in any way superior to or more highly evolved than an ape.

Any theory of human evolution, any story that tries to explain why we became different from the apes, is automatically a story of our most basic nature. And, for me, a story of our nature needs to ring true and be like a key that solves all kinds of mysteries. I doubt that we will ever have enough facts or be able to test and clearly demonstrate our nature as animals. I think we'll always have to settle for a story—be it myth, legend or scientific theory. And what I want is a good story, the best I can come up with. This is why the running hypothesis still intrigues me. It says that we became upright in order to breathe better, in order to increase our stamina and endurance. In order that we might have more spirit and consciousness.

carpenter

At a particularly low point in my career as a responsible husband and father, I worked as a carpenter's assistant for my younger brother, a contractor specializing in home renovation. We built additions and garages, finished basements, tore out bathrooms and installed new ones, and so on. He paid me ten dollars an hour, which I considered to be generous. At that time good carpenters—men who could build an entire house, from start to finish, single-handed—were making twelve-fifty, and I was only an assistant, a gopher, the guy who digs and carries and cleans up.

My brother was thirty-two at the time and had worked as a carpenter since he'd graduated from college. He'd been a good student and was offered a graduate fellowship, but he'd dropped it, and no one in my family really understood why. He went to work for other people and eventually got his own license and enough equipment to start getting his own contracts. He had a lot of work, usually two jobs going at once, and three or four employees, but he wasn't making much money because he had a tendency to underestimate the bids. I think sometimes I ended up making more on a job than he did, but he seemed to like it anyway.

I, however, was almost always upset; not because the work was hard, but because I resented working on another man's house—a man with enough money to pay for a $40,000 bathroom. A man who decides he wants a bigger garage for his new motorcycle. A man who doesn't want to dig up his own sewer pipe. The work forced me to admit that I was a slave; that somewhere in life I'd made a big mistake.

Also, I had a problem with the other carpenters my brother hired. Consider the following scenarios:

I am shingling a garage roof with a lead carpenter named Dave. It's Dave's first day on the job, and we are both up there pounding shingles and talking about *Star Trek*. Dave is a big *Star Trek* fan, he's seen all of the old and new shows and even has floor plans of the U.S.S. *Enterprise*, which he has committed to memory. Dave tells me about the insidious Borg, a race of cyborgs with the social conscience of ants; Dave knows why the Klingons are now part of the Federation; and Dave has decided just how he would spend his time on the Holodeck, a room on the *Enterprise* where crew members go to live out their fantasies in holographic reality. It's harmless conversation that seems to diminish the tedium of the work. But then, after a brief lull, Dave stops pounding shingles and asks me in a very serious tone, "Scott, have you accepted Christ as your personal savior?" Turns out Dave is a fundamentalist Christian with a strong desire to proselytize. That evening after work I ask my brother if maybe he doesn't need a foundation dug or some fiberglass insulation stapled in place, anything other than working with Dave. He looks at the ground and kicks the dirt and says he promised the owner that the roof would be done last week.

After Dave there is Steve, who tells me about how, in Idaho, they are implanting silicon chips in babies' ankles that will forever identify them as part of Satan's army. After Steve there is another Dave, who, when he's alone, practices out loud, shouting, his sermons exposing the evils of the Tri-lateralist Commission. And after that Dave there is John, who my brother hires as a grunt to help me out. John has just arrived from Boston where he drove a cab for twenty years up until the Kennedys ran him out of town. He says Ted Kennedy was out to get him. He says Ted Kennedy has ruined his life. And he tells me the amazing story of how, while hitchhiking west through Kansas, he became so depressed he decided to throw himself in front of a semi-truck barreling down I-70. But then, suddenly from out of nowhere, he saw Jesus Christ standing forty feet tall on the side of the road. Jesus spoke to him. He said, "John, these trucks are my roller skates."

When you see a thing happen once it's an accident; when you see it happen twice it's a coincidence; and when you see it three or more times it's a science, and science demands theories. My first theory was that there might be some sort of connection between Jesus and these men because they were all carpenters. And so I would ask my work-mates questions like, "Was Jesus a framer or a finish man? I mean it makes a difference, don't you think? Was he the lead carpenter, or was he just a laborer?" Or I'd make up stuff, like, "I heard that when Jesus built furniture he never used glue in the joints, that he'd just touch them and they'd hold forever."

But these men were not interested in philosophy or metaphysics. And they were not even interested, it turned out, in stories about Jesus or his teachings of compassion. Far from it. They were all into the Book of Revelation; they were all religious for reasons of revenge. They had had hard lives filled with injustices and inequities and had resigned themselves to a life over which they had lost control. Their one hope was that when they die, when everyone dies, everyone will get what they deserve. The righteous will be happy forever, while "the bastards," "the assholes," "the wicked and corrupt" and "the filth" will burn in hell.

So I changed my theory and decided that religion is something people use not only because they want to connect with a sense of their spiritual existence, but to bring a sense of justice to their social exis-tence—just wait until Jesus comes back, just wait until the Apoca-lypse. I thought, at first, that I was different, even superior, to these guys, but at some point I started to realize that we all had the same basic problem: we were all slaves, unhappy slaves. It wasn't a pretty thing to see.

I went on like this for more than a year, angry and depressed, and unable or unwilling to do anything else. And then one day in the mid-dle of the winter everything came to a head and sort of exploded. We were building a three-story addition onto the back of an architect's home. He'd designed it, and we'd framed the thing and were starting to sheet the roof when a building inspector came by and said we'd screwed up, made a mistake down at the level of the foundation. It was a small thing, a trivial thing. I can't even remember now specifically what the problem was. And then, we hadn't done anything wrong. We'd built it like it was drawn in the plans, and the architect was happy with our work. But it just didn't quite match the city's building code and the inspector was being a hard-ass. He said we'd have to fix it, which meant that we'd have to tear down the whole thing and start over.

I was standing there in the mud with my brother and the inspector. It was snowing, and I was wet and cold and couldn't believe what I was hearing. My brother just listened and didn't argue or protest, and the inspector showed no sign of regret. He filled out a form and gave it to my brother and left. I was furious. I took off my belt and threw it across the yard, nails and screws and tools scattering and disappearing in the snow.

John stopped working and came over, and I told him we were going to have to take down everything. He started in about the Kennedys, how he knew a lawyer in Boston, how he knew we could sue the inspector for everything he was worth. I told him to shut the fuck up, and asked my brother what we were going to do. He was standing inside on the bottom floor looking out through an empty window, and he said, quite calmly, "Mark your time cards for a full day, and let's clean up and go home early." If he was mad, I couldn't see it.

We put everything away, and just as I was leaving he said, "Thanks. It'll be all right. I'll go down to city hall tomorrow and talk to some people." I got in my car and loaded my pipe and smoked a bowl and drove away. It was still snowing and cars were sliding into the gutters and getting stuck, and I was trying to figure out why I was so pissed while my brother seemed so unfazed. After all, he would have to pay us to do the extra work. The money would come out of his pocket, not ours. Then I realized that it was his life, that he'd chosen to do this, and he didn't hate it. He didn't hate anything about it.

I drove downtown and went into the shopping mall and bought a new pair of work boots, good boots with good leather and good support. I paid $125 for them and wore them out of the store and left my old wet shoes on top of a phone booth on the street.

hitchhike

She cried and drove away, leaving me standing on the east-bound side of I–80 in a light snow flurry, the cars and trucks ripping up the wet road like the tearing of nylon. Leaving Salt Lake City. Again. There was a problem with money—specifically, that I hadn't been making very much of it. But there was also the promise of money from a publisher in New York, and it was her idea that I go to New York, get the money and come back before the mortgage was late, again; before she went insane altogether. She wanted me to fly, but there was no money to fly, so I said I would hitchhike. I said I could hitchhike a thousand miles a day, and I could, at least I used to be able to. But the minute I got out of the car I realized that I was too old for it now. Twenty-two hundred miles across the country in the middle of December? What was I thinking?

I closed my mind and stuck out my thumb.

In two easy-to-get rides I was in Cheyenne, Wyoming—the gray weather gone and the sky opened up big and blue, three inches of snow the high desert prairie. It was two-thirty in the afternoon and the sun was almost setting, throwing long shadows out in front of the big trucks gliding by almost silently at eighty-five miles an hour. It was the edge of my turf, the end of the mountains. From there it would be the high plains and the low plains and the rivers, and then Chicago. I shuddered to think of Chicago—all steel and brick and the squeal of freight trains in the night. I shuddered to think of the long tollways, the dark pipeline, to the East Coast.

When I was young, hitchhiking was fun. I could hitchhike faster than I could drive myself, and everyone who picked me up would spill their guts and tell me what happened to them. There was simply no better way to see and know America. You may laugh, but it's true. For example, there was the time I found myself at the airport in Salmon, Idaho, 150 miles from my car in Stanley. I got a ride with a young kid who said he was a world-class surfer and, after talking to him for a while, I believed him. He had some "Kuwaiti Blue" marijuana that we smoked in a gravel pit just off the road, and then he showed me a floating disk of ice, about thirty feet in diameter, that spun around and around in the Salmon River. "It's there in the same place every winter," he said. "We take acid, man, and go out there in the full moon and just kick back and look at the sky." I didn't know whether to believe that or not, but it was a beautiful image. After he let me out at his grandmother's house I got a ride with a lonely vacuum sales-man—kind of creepy. Then, as I was walking through Challis, a woman with two kids in her car gave me a ride to the end of town. She gave me her phone number and said, "If you don't get a ride before dark you can stay with us. It's so cold out." I didn't get a ride, and so I called and her husband came to pick me up and I spent the night with her family. It turned out she was dying from bone cancer. She'd been through years of treatments and had given up on the idea of recovery. Her husband, her young son and daughter tried to be cheerful, but you could see that every day for them was full of heartache and pain. Before I went to sleep on her living-room floor I asked her why she'd picked me up, and she quoted a line from the Bible about not turning away a stranger because you never know if he might be an angel. I told her I was no angel, and she said, "I know, you just looked like a nice man who was trying to get somewhere."

If I had not been hitchhiking, if I had driven the same stretch in my car, then I would never have seen the ice disk; I would not know that Eureka makes the most popular vacuum in central Idaho; and I would not have been shown this compassion from a woman who was look-ing at her kids and husband for maybe the last time—I would have seen the Sawtooth Mountains at sunset, but I would not have these memories to go with it.

And yet, standing on the side of the road in Cheyenne, Wyoming, I knew things had changed, and that I should be moving on to another phase of my life. When I was younger, I had nothing to lose—no sense of myself as someone who *shouldn't* be standing on the side of the road. But somehow I'd picked up some self-importance along the way, and I needed to lose it. Quickly. There was no time for self-pity. In an hour and a half, it would be dark, and then I'd have to spend the night with Earl Holding's emperor penguin in the lobby of Little America, which would be absolutely no fun at all.

I watched a semi coming toward me, and I didn't even bother to hold up my hand, as truckers usually can't take riders. But the driver threw up his arms like, "What, are you hitchhiking or not?" I jumped and yelled, and he hit the brakes and pulled over about a quarter mile down the road.

It was a new Volvo, spotless, with bunk beds, a refrigerator, a television, and a five-disc CD player. The driver was a big guy—over six feet tall and more than 250 pounds. "I didn't think truckers could pick up hitchhikers because of their insurance," I said.

"This is my truck, I can do what I want," he said. I told him I was going to New York, and he said that he had a load of floor safes to drop in Illinois and Pennsylvania but that he was ultimately headed for his girlfriend's house in Somerville, New Jersey, which was only about thirty miles from Manhattan. "You're welcome to come as long as you keep up your end of the conversation and help me stay awake," he said. "I like to drive pretty much straight through if I can."

His name was Zarko Jurisic, a Serb from Belgrade, although he'd lived in the United States since 1980 and spoke English with only a slight accent. He wanted me to know, in no uncertain terms, that the former Yugoslavia was ruined by greed and corruption and that the Yugoslavians themselves are to blame. "Yep!" he said, shouting, "we fucked it up about as well as anyone could. It'll take two thousand years for it to recover." I thought about asking him why the Serbs seem to be such coldhearted murderers, but then I thought about

Chicago and kept my mouth shut. Anyway, he was an American now, having taken the oath last year.

He wanted to know, of course, who I was and why I was going to New York. I told him I was a writer, and he asked, "What kind of a writer? I mean have you had anything published? Forgive me for saying so, but it seems kind of odd for you to be hitchhiking if you are a successful writer." I told him that I had in fact been offered a book contract from a publisher in New York and that I was going there to pick up some of the money.

"But I would think that as a writer you would know how to use the telephone and the Federal Express, or don't they do things that way in your business?"

"Yeah, sure, but sometimes the checks have a way of not getting mailed," I said. "And I figured that by going there I could speed things up a bit."

He thought about that for a minute, and I was hoping that he would think I was just making it all up and let it slide. Then he reached for a compartment over his head and pulled out a stack of pamphlets.

"Here," he said, "I want to show you something."

I immediately stiffened, thinking he was a born-again Christian and that I will have to spend my time in hell.

"Look at these and tell me what you see."

The pamphlets were advertisements for the paintings of his cousin, Vojislav Jurisic, who still lived in Belgrade. The paintings were portraits and Biblical scenes done in the style of Rembrandt. The title of the pamphlet was "Undiscovered Masterpieces."

"This is the name of my art gallery, Undiscovered Masterpieces. It's the bottom floor of my house. I have devoted the entire space to my cousin's work because he is a great artist, better, I believe, than Picasso. I am helping him seek the credit he most definitely deserves."

I looked some more at the paintings. The best ones were the Biblical scenes: Abraham, knife raised, ready to sacrifice his son, Isaac; the creation of Eve, her body taking shape from a cloud while being encircled by the snake; Moses with the stone tablet, the words of the commandments in flames.

"But this stuff is way out of fashion," I said. "I can see how they would be hard to sell."

"It never went out of fashion, my friend," Zarko said, poking at me and just missing my shoulder. "It never (poke) went out (poke) of fashion (poke). You can't deny the presence (poke) of the human spirit on the canvas. It's either there or it isn't."

"Yes, but these photographs are kind of small. It's hard to get a good feel for them."

"We will go to my house in Hazelton, Pennsylvania, and you can see for yourself," he said. "You can stand in front to the paintings and study your own reactions and tell me in your own opinion, 'Zarko, you are really full of shit,' or, 'Man, this is spirituality through art; this is truly the work of a genius who sees the eternal forms through inspiration.'"

This is the way it happens sometimes in hitchhiking. You're going along, minding your own business, and then suddenly you become stuck in somebody else's life. I didn't really want to go to Zarko's house and look at his cousin's paintings, because then he would expect me to write a glorious review of the work that might make him famous. I told him that I doubted that I could do anything to help him, that I didn't know a thing about art and wouldn't know how to write a story about his cousin's work. But he wouldn't take no for an answer. I was in his truck and I was going to his house, that's all there was to it.

The sun went down as we entered Nebraska, and the road straightened out to the point where Zarko could steer with his knees and do things like read a map and change the CD without looking at the road. The truck was so high tech I think it could have steered itself. It was a smooth ride, and we were listening to Brahms, arguing politely a dialogue on aesthetics.

"The man who wrote this music was a great artist," Zarko said. "He saw the eternal forms and then wrote this symphony."

"Yes," I said, "certainly. But what, dear Zarko, *are* the eternal forms? Do they have substance? Or are they only ideas? And are they comprehendible to all or only a few?"

"They exist as substance," he said. "You see them in the sunset, you hear them in music, you see them in the great masterpieces of art. But they also exist beyond substance, in a way that is both mysterious and frightening. I have seen them; I would even go so far as to say that I have been inspired by them—and I think everyone is capable of having this experience—but it is only a few people, only the great masters, who can turn this inspiration into a work of art."

"And what is a work of art?" I asked.

"A work of art is something that speaks to us," Zarko said. "It says, 'We *are* going somewhere. Have faith. We just need to learn to use this stuff—these bodies and these minds.' You will see. You will stand in front of my cousin's paintings and see for yourself, the man is truly a great master."

After 500 miles we pulled off at a truck stop near Omaha and parked with 200 other diesel engines, side by side, idling through the night like an army of sleeping dragons. Zarko turned on the heater and gave me the top bunk, and it was so hot I couldn't sleep. I looked out the little window by my head and saw another truck stop on the other side of the freeway that I remembered from having been there many years ago, also at night, also in December, hitchhiking home from New York. I'd flown back to the States from India. I landed with a hundred dollars and went immediately to Macy's and bought a pair of basketball shoes for sixty bucks, and then caught a bus to New Jersey. I remembered that I didn't think it was a big deal then to hitchhike across the country with less than forty dollars. I remembered I got stuck at the truck stop on the other side of the road, so I laid down in my sleeping bag on the entrance ramp, and a trucker stopped and yelled at me, "What the hell are you doing? I thought you were dead! Come on, get in." He gave me a ride all the way to Salt Lake.

I remembered a thousand-mile ride through the Yukon Territory with a guy who listened to an instructional tape on turkey calling for what seemed like the entire trip. I remembered the jail in Goodland,

Kansas; a long cold ride across the basin and range with a paranoid insurance salesman running away from home in Providence, Rhode Island. I remembered rides from two decades of wandering around, until I wore myself out and fell asleep.

We got up in the morning and drove straight into the sun. I missed the Missouri River for the glare. Zarko was driving like he was all of a sudden in a hurry, tailgating a poor commuter on his way to work in Council Bluffs. He was doing eighty in a sixty-five-mile-an-hour zone, and a highway patrolman pulled him over and gave him the third degree, asking for his registration, his logbook, fuel receipts and proof that he stopped at the weigh station on the Utah/Wyoming border. Then the cop saw my backpack behind the seat and asked me what my story was. I told him I was going to New York. He asked for my driver's license and told Zarko to come sit with him in his cruiser.

Zarko came back forty-five minutes later with one citation for a logbook infraction and another for carrying an unauthorized passenger.

"What about the speeding?" I asked.

"He let it go, saying he was doing me a favor so I wouldn't get points on my license, but I told him, 'Please, don't insult my intelligence; these stops are not about speeding. You don't need 1,100 troopers to enforce the speed limit. I come from my own country. I know how you guys operate. It's all about money. So go ahead, take my money, but don't insult my intelligence.'"

"Did he check my license?"

"Yeah, he had a computer and a phone, and he made two calls to Utah—one to see if I stopped at the weigh station—which, as far as I'm concerned, it turns out they lost the record of my being there—and another to check to see if you are a wanted criminal. It turns out you forgot to take out the garbage last week, but other than that you're clean. Still, it's against the law, even in my own truck, for me to give you a ride. He told me to drop you at the next exit, and I told him I wouldn't even consider it. This country is becoming a police state. I know, I've seen it all before."

We dropped half of the floor safes at a warehouse in a cornfield in the middle of Illinois and then drove north to get back on I–80 near the edge of the black hole of Chicago. We ate dinner at a truck stop just before the tollway, and I tried to pick up the tab, but Zarko insisted that neither one of us was paying because they didn't have any meat in the buffet. Two security guards followed us out into the parking lot, telling us to come back, but Zarko was as big as both of them put together and he was saying, "Go ahead, call the cops, I'll tell them about your lousy service." We got in the truck and looked down on them standing in front of us like they were going to block our exit, but Zarko just stuck it in gear and pulled away. That was the best way I'd ever passed by Chicago.

The next day we dropped the rest of the floor safes at a warehouse in a forest in Pennsylvania and then drove another eighty miles south to a parking lot behind a shopping mall to trade the empty trailer for one filled with pillows for a Wal-Mart in Michigan. Zarko had me switch the trailers so that I could learn a new skill in case my writing career bottomed out. Then we drove north to Hazelton, to Zarko's home and the Undiscovered Masterpieces Art Gallery, arriving at midnight.

It was an old two-story brick building that used to be a grocery store and then a pizza parlor. Zarko lived upstairs with his mother and his sister and her little girl. His sister was out and the girl was asleep, but his mother was up watching *Mad Max* on cable. We had a couple of beers and then went downstairs for the moment of truth.

Zarko had obviously spent a lot of money fixing the room to look like an art gallery—good lights, the walls painted white, the large paintings hung neatly spaced apart. I stood in front of the Biblical scenes for an extended period of time, looking from close-up and a few steps back, trying to see the presence of the eternal forms on the canvas. Zarko stood in a corner by the door, not saying a word.

The paintings were the kind that tries to make you believe in God, and that he's really pissed off at just about everybody, which I didn't and don't believe. If there is a God, then he's having a really good time.

He's happy about everything. I'm pretty sure on that. But the paintings *were* intense, and finely done. The longer I looked, the more it seemed that Abraham, Eve, and the snake were becoming three-dimensional, like they were coming out into the room.

"Your cousin may be a truly great genius," I said, "but it seems like he might be insane as well. He paints like he has fire in his eyes and lightning shooting out of his fingertips."

"Yes, it's true, he does," Zarko says. "He is a difficult man. We've spoken many times on the telephone, even while the United States was bombing Belgrade. I could hear the bombs exploding in the background. He gets upset that I haven't sold any of his paintings. He accuses me of being lazy and stupid. But I tell him, 'Be patient, I'm making contacts in the art world, and these things take some time.'"

"How much does he want for them?" I ask.

"For the larger ones, between one and two hundred thousand dollars."

"It seems like a lot," I said, "but I suppose if you were rich, and wanted one, then it would be nothing."

Zarko looked at the floor.

"They are good, though." I didn't really know what to say—the Old Testament done in the Dutch Baroque by a modern-day Serb and hung in a former pizza parlor in Hazelton, Pennsylvania, by a truck driver . . . this seemed beyond my ability for comment.

The next morning we drove to Somerville, New Jersey, where Zarko's girlfriend lived. He found the train station, and I shook his hand and told him thanks, but it was kind of hard to get out of his car—you ride across the country with someone and then it's like, "O.K., thanks, see ya." It wasn't enough, and left me feeling empty, like splitting after a one-night stand. Yet another reason why I was too old to hitchhike.

I waited twenty-five minutes for the train to come—a longer period of time than I'd waited, all combined, on the side of the road. I sat down and gave the conductor some money and looked out the window at the narrow streets and beat-up shops on the other side of the continent. The country seemed so small—so easy to close the distance. I still had sixty dollars in my pocket and two clean shirts in my backpack. The train eventually dropped into a tunnel under the Hudson River, and New York City was mine.

1993

The pronghorn is the sole survivor of a vast number of pronghorn-like species that existed during the past 10 million years. Since the pleistocene epoch, about a million years ago, all of these strange and fantastic pronghorns have vanished except antilocapra americana, which is believed to have changed very little since then. For a million years it has roamed the plains and deserts of North America in substantially the same form.

Joe Van Wormer, *The World of the Pronghorn* (Philadelphia: J. B. Lippincott, 1969), pp. 15–16.

Neither the animals nor I believe in the city. There is no boundary that wilderness does not cross. I see a peregrine falcon in the tree outside our bedroom window. I see moose on Black Mountain, a mile from the city. I read in the paper how a cougar was trapped downtown. I see bald eagles over the cemetery; a big horned owl sitting on top of a telephone pole at midnight, looking for house cats. Every evening there are winds out of the canyons—Red Butte, Emigration and City Creek. There are coyotes in City Creek, coyotes up and down the canyon calling to each other at sunset.

I've read everything I can find in the university library that's been written on pronghorns, which really isn't all that much. They're still somewhat mysterious animals, even to the scientists who study them. If my brother's theory is correct—that evolution of the species moves toward greater stamina and endurance—then pronghorn antelope are among the most highly evolved creatures on the planet. They metabolize oxygen at a rate three and a half times higher than even the finest human runners. They have twice as much blood, and their hearts and lungs are three times the size of a mammal of comparable weight. They can run the equivalent of a marathon in forty minutes, and can easily maintain a speed of forty miles per hour for more than sixty minutes. They have no body fat whatsoever.

According to Stan Linstedt, a biologist at Northern Arizona University in Flagstaff, Arizona, the pronghorn are the best endurance athletes in the world. I called and talked with him for a while, and he told me the individual animals he studies were raised from young fawns in his lab, and that they are as affectionate as house dogs. He hugs them every morning when he comes to work. "They're really cool animals."

In 1850 there were 60 million pronghorn antelope in North America, but they were nearly wiped out along with the buffalo, and there are only about a million left today. They are said to have 10x vision, which means that on a clear night they can see the rings of Saturn. Their eye sockets are positioned on the outermost part of the skull, looking sideways as much as forward, and so they can see almost 360 degrees. They are the only horned animal in the world that sheds its horns, and the only one whose horns are branched or pronged. They eat mainly sagebrush, but also rabbitbrush, salt sage, winter fat, four-wing saltbrush, scarlet globemallow and fireweed summer cypress. I'm trying to learn what these plants look like.

When I drive across the desert I look for pronghorn standing by the highway. One time, on I–80 in Wyoming, I saw three of them outrun a freight train. In northwestern Nevada there was a large herd of fifty that ran alongside my car—they flew out ahead and across the road like a river flowing sixty miles an hour. Again in Wyoming, at night, I saw what looked like a cluster of luminescent grapes along the road, and then realized it was the eyes of a group of pronghorn, hanging out and watching the traffic like it was a drive-in movie. And then in the Great Salt Lake Desert, I saw a lone male standing motionless and staring while four F–16 fighter jets flew low over its head on their way to the bombing range. Pronghorn love speed and fast things, and they're maybe too curious for their own good.

I've been watching that lone male for a couple of years now. He's part of a small herd that I can always find in a place called Puddle Valley, a no-man's-land just west of the Great Salt Lake—east of the Bonneville Salt Flats, south of the Hill Air Force Bombing Range, and north of the Dugway Proving Grounds where the army tests biological and chemical weapons. There's one paved road that runs up the valley, and the antelope are nearly always standing alongside the road, if not right on the asphalt itself. They'll walk slowly away if I stop and get out of the car, but otherwise they just stand there and look at me, only thirty yards away.

I've been thinking that this herd would be a lot easier to chase than the herds in Wyoming because there are so few of them, and then I've been watching the lone male enough that I think I could recognize him at a distance. His horns are shaped like a heart and he has a brown line on his chest that curls around like a question mark. I call him "the lone male" because I have only once seen him with the others in his herd, and this was in the fall when he was rutting with two does, going from one to the other with a hard-on, barking and kicking up dirt, pissing and shitting and marking plants with the scent gland on his cheek.

Once, in the early spring, I saw him through binoculars from a half-mile away. He was looking right back at me, and so I knelt down a bit with my head just below his line of sight. I waited for ten minutes and stood up, slowly, and he was standing there looking at me, only a quarter of a mile away. So I sat down and waited, and he came to within a hundred yards. I lay flat and could hear him in the sagebrush barking at me, like a sharp cough. He came real close, less than thirty yards away, and I stood up, and he didn't take off. He just stood there and barked at me and scratched the dirt with his front leg and then slowly wandered off.

a trip to cambodia

I came to my office late at night, and the offer was on the phone machine: four days in Cambodia, all expenses paid, in exchange for a story to be aired on a new public radio travel show. The sponsor of the trip was the very famous Raffles International Hotel Company, which I'd never heard of. Could I leave in two days? I glanced at my Union Pacific calendar, blank for the entire month. All I knew about Cambodia was that we bombed it during the Vietnam War. I remembered President Nixon explaining, on television, that we needed to do this because the North Vietnamese were using Cambodia as a staging area for their assaults on South Vietnam. I remembered that four students had been gunned down at Kent State for protesting the bombing. I'd seen *The Killing Fields* and understood that after the Vietnam War the Khmer Rouge had instigated a communist revolution in Cambodia, where more than a million people had died. But that was over twenty years ago. It might be a very nice place by now. I called back and left a message saying my bag was already packed.

There were five of us on the trip. The others were all professional travel writers from such publications as *Town and Country* and *National Geographic Traveler*. We flew business class on a 747 with lots of legroom and private televisions that came up out of the armrests. We were served wine, exotic fruit juices, salmon and lobster. Every so often the steward came by with a hot towel for my hands and face. The flight took twenty hours, so I had some time to read up on Raffles, and their operations, and the current conditions in Cambodia.

Raffles International specializes in renovating grand hotels, the

Raffles House in Singapore being the most famous. The company had recently renovated two French colonialist hotels in Cambodia—the Hotel Le Royal in Phnom Penh and Le Grand Hotel d'Ankgor in Siem Riep, a small town near the ancient temples of the Angkor civilization. Unfortunately, almost nobody had been visiting Cambodia lately. The previous summer, just as the millions of dollars of renovations in both hotels were being completed, the Cambodian government went to war with itself. There were tanks squaring off in the streets shooting at each other, and bombs had exploded at the airport, leaving holes in the runway and blood spattered on the walls of the terminal building. Tourists and foreign aid officials couldn't get out of the country fast enough. They fled in C–1 transport planes brought in by the Thai air force. Since then, tourism in Cambodia had dwindled to a small number of young European, Japanese and American backpackers with nowhere near enough money to stay at a Raffles hotel.

We were met at the airport in Phnom Penh by the manager of the Hotel Le Royal, a suave British expatriate with an expensive suit and perfect hair. We rode into town in an air-conditioned BMW limousine, looking out at the mass of people, the rundown buildings wrapped in a chaotic web of phone wires, the streets covered with a thick pad of light brown dirt. I asked about the current political situation, and the manager said that the country was remarkably calm and stable, that there had been a perceived negativism in the press lately, which was regrettable and unfortunate. "The city itself," he said, "hasn't been as peaceful and safe in a long time. It's all really very encouraging, very encouraging."

My room at Le Royal was the Charles de Gaulle Suite. It had real Persian rugs, wall-to-wall marble in the bathroom, furniture made from beautiful hardwood—luxurious. I turned on the cable television and watched the second "Ghostbusters" film. I flipped to CNBC and watched a weather report for all of Asia—cloudy in Lhasa, snow in Beijing, ninety-five degrees in Singapore.

I was scheduled to have lunch and then tour the hotel with the other writers, but I was determined to skip the dog and pony show. I realized that my absence would be considered to be an act of disrespect, but I was not a travel writer and did not want to be a travel writer, which I considered to be only a step or two above prostitution. I'd accepted the job as a one-time deal, thinking that I could write and produce a story on my own terms, a story about the real Cambodia, a country that was relatively unknown at that time. I thought it was my obligation to do this. So I walked out of the hotel and, for the equivalent of fifteen cents, got into a cyclo headed south down Monivong Boulevard.

A "cyclo" is a goofy tricycle rickshaw taxi where you sit down low to the ground with your feet sticking out into the oncoming traffic. There seemed to be no question of whether to drive in the right or left lane, there was just the road, which was like a river flowing in both directions at once—cars, cyclos, motorcycles and trucks making their way at breakneck speeds through whatever space was available at the moment. The only traffic rule seemed to be that the bigger vehicle had the right of way.

I asked the driver to stop at Lucky Lucky Motorcycle Rentals, where I spoke with Mr. Lucky. I knew that in order to get away from the group I would have to have my own transportation, and I thought a large, fast motorcycle would be the perfect vehicle. Mr. Lucky recommended a 250cc Yamaha dirt bike, and I agreed. I asked Mr. Lucky if it would be all right with him if I rode the bike up Highway 6 to Siem Riep, the next stop on the tour, two hundred miles to the northeast. The other writers were going to fly there, but I much preferred driving as this would allow me to see the countryside and perhaps meet some typical Cambodians. Mr. Lucky said I could take the bike cross-country, but that I would have to leave my passport with him, and that I should be very careful to avoid the police and any military personnel I might see along the way. He said that I shouldn't stop for them under any circumstance, as this would be quite dangerous. He also recommended that I ride as fast as possible and stop only if it was absolutely necessary. I gave him my passport and rode out into the river of traffic.

I knew it was a mistake to have coughed up my passport, but I preferred the possible risk of haggling with the authorities rather than accepting the certainty of being trapped inside the decadent graces of the six-star tour. And yet, I was concerned enough about what Mr. Lucky had said that I decided I'd better get a second opinion. So I consulted my Lonely Planet guidebook and found the address of the United Nations office. I rode over there and asked to speak to the security officer.

He was French, six feet tall and over 250 pounds, wearing a gold necklace and sweating profusely as his office had no air-conditioning. It was late in the afternoon and he acted a little put out, but I told him I'd just arrived and figured he would be the best source for information. "Is there someone in town who is more knowledgeable than yourself?" I asked.

"No, of course not," he said. "I have continual telephone communication with representatives in all the outlying areas. What is it that you want to know?"

I asked him if he thought it was safe to ride a motorcycle to Siem Riep, and he laughed and said, "Only a fool would think so." He told me there were only three cities in the entire country where tourists were safe—Phnom Penh, Siem Riep and Sianookville—and that even in these places there had been some trouble. "Of course I can't tell you what to do," he said, "but I highly recommend that you fly to Siem Riep. The countryside is ruled by the Khmer Rouge and other rival factions, and all of them have guns, a lot of guns. They will take you as a hostage for ransom or just shoot you straight out and take your motorcycle."

"So no tourists travel on the highways?" I asked.

"Yes, there are those who do, and there are those who have been killed. Others seem to have no problems. If you insist on going this way you should be alert to such things as, for instance, if all of a sudden the traffic stops or if the road suddenly becomes empty. These are signs that something may be wrong. If you are stopped and detained by someone with a weapon, give him twenty or thirty dollars. Give him whatever he wants. People are shot because they resist."

Then he said he'd like to visit with me some more but, as it was five o'clock, he would be leaving. Perhaps, if I wanted more information, I should talk with the journalists who hang out at the Foreign Correspondents Club. "Wait until nine or ten this evening," he said. "They will all be there. You can count on it."

I rode back to the hotel and was met in the lobby by the Raffles public relations man who had organized the trip. He'd been very friendly up to this point, but he'd been waiting for me and was visibly upset.

"Where have you been?" he said, as if I were an errant teenager. "What are you doing with that motorcycle?" I told him I very much appreciated being invited on the tour, but that in order to write a story I needed other sources of information. "Listen, Scott," he said. "Our company has paid a considerable sum of money to bring you here, and I think we have a right to demand that you attend to our schedule. Everyone is very upset with you, especially the director. He feels personally responsible for your safety."

"But your manager claims the city is safe now," I said. "Is this true or not? You can't expect me to write a story recommending that people come to Cambodia when it's not safe to leave the hotel. I can't do that, regardless of how much money your company has spent."

"So where did you go? Who did you speak with?"

I told him I had been to the United Nations office and briefly summarized what the security officer had said, which made him come undone.

"I will have to call your executive producer," he said. "And you will have to speak with the director. Your behavior is completely unprofessional."

"Yes," I said, "it's fine with me if you call my boss, and I'd like to speak with the director. I have a lot of questions I'd like to ask him. Is he available now?"

"No, he's still at his office in Singapore, but he's coming to meet us in Siem Riep in a couple of days. He's a very busy man, and he's a good man with the best intentions. He took enormous risks to renovate these hotels. If something were to happen to you while under his supervision, there would be very serious consequences for everyone involved, don't you see?"

"Yes, I see. But I'm wondering if you're more worried about my safety or what I might find out by speaking with other people."

At that point he gave up arguing, saying that he would set up an appointment with the director, and walked away.

The Foreign Correspondents Club was a bar on the third floor of a building overlooking the Tonle Sap River near its confluence with the Mekong. One entire wall of the bar was open from floor to ceiling, providing a beautiful view of the water and the traffic flowing by on the boulevard below. There was a good sound-system playing a sort of mesmerizing, ethereal pop music, and the place was packed with Western men and women, young and happy, sitting in comfortable leather lounge chairs, drinking beer and smoking marijuana. It was a great place, perhaps the best bar I'd ever been in. I asked the bartender if he knew any journalists in the house, and he made a sweeping motion with his arm as if to say they were all journalists. So I asked him for the best journalist, and he pointed to a man sitting in a lounge chair holding court with six or seven others.

I went over and introduced myself and pled for mercy in the face of my ignorance and then boldly asked for a briefing. I had used this tactic in bars in Nevada and Wyoming only to have met with the gravest of consequences. But in Phnom Penh it worked. I was taken in by Ed Fitzgerald, a Canadian, who had worked as an NBC correspondent until the company had been sold to General Electric, whereupon he accepted a large severance package and set up his own company in Phnom Penh, producing stories for the Asia Business News and CNBC's "Asia Report."

"The king," he said, "Norodom Sihanook, fled the country in January fearing for his life and is now living in Beijing. The prince, Norodom Rinaridh, fled one day before the military coup last July, and is now living in Paris. His royalist military forces are hiding in the jungle and some are now said to be allied with the Khmer Rouge. Since July, foreign aid, which once comprised sixty percent of the Cambodian federal budget, has disappeared. The current economy is jungle-based—the money being primarily in hardwood and heroin."

I told him that the bartender had said that he was the best journalist in the house, and he laughed and said that this was due most likely to a story he produced about how the Cambodian government and the Khmer Rouge are enemies in war but partners in the heroin trade, moving six hundred kilograms of the drug out of the capital every month. "After the story aired, everyone thought I would be assassinated," he said, chuckling. "They say I have a magic vest—you know, like Crazy Horse, that bullets can't penetrate."

"Well, why do you think you're still alive?" I asked.

"People in power here are smart enough to realize that killing me would only make things harder on themselves. What they want, more than anything right now, is to join the parade, the new world economy. They know that this is where the real money is. And then, there are just so many other problems.

"In Cambodia," he said, "one out of ten babies die at birth. In Cambodia, one out of five children die before the age of five. Sixty percent of the population is under the age of twenty-six. This is a country, the size of the state of Missouri, on which the United States dropped 600,000 tons of bombs from 1969 to 1973. This is a country that then went through a communist revolution where 1.5 million people, a quarter of the population, were tortured and murdered or died from starvation and disease . . . a country where there are now less than 10 million alive but more than 10 million land mines still in the ground. I know thousands of amputees," he said. "Thousands."

I was speechless and wanted to go out on the veranda for some air and maybe look at the river for a while, but Fitzgerald wasn't through.

"I think you should tell people to come to Cambodia," he said.

"The more who see it the better. Tourism is a good thing—it brings in dollars and it brings in people who see how bad things are, and then they go home and talk about it. And this is, after all, a very beautiful country. The people, even after all they've been through, are warm and passionate and very friendly to tourists. I think you should tell people to come here but that they should be smart about it. Don't come to Cambodia and rent a motorcycle and head off down the highway. This is not a country for the unwary. This is not Tahiti; this is not Bali. You can die here—if not by being taken hostage and shot, then by just stepping off the road to take a leak."

I rode home at 2:00 A.M. and the streets were absolutely deserted. The Frenchman had said this was a sign that something might be wrong, and I realized what was wrong was that I was lost. I rode in the direction I felt good about, and then in some other directions I felt increasingly less good about, and then, finally, I saw it, all lit up and glowing from within—the Hotel Le Royal, one of the finest hotels in one of the worst places in the world.

The next morning I decided to stick with the group. We went first to the Royal Palace, but nobody was home. Then we went to a Christian mission that ran a handicrafts center which employed handicapped people—mostly kids who'd been hit by land mines. They showed us how they make baskets, even a thirteen-year-old boy who'd had his eyes blown out and the skin crudely sewn shut with a big X over each eye socket. Then they played a song for us—a young, one-armed boy playing the drum, a girl missing a foot on the Cambodian tror.

After lunch we had a choice. We could either (a) relax at the spa and have a massage; (b) visit a famous artist's studio; or (c) go on a tour of the killing fields. Three of us, the three men, chose the killing fields, which was actually just one of the many, many killing fields in Cambodia. They'd made this particular one into a memorial park.

But first we stopped at the Toul Sleng Prison. Before Pol Pot and the Khmer Rouge took over in 1975, the prison had been a junior high school. More than 14,000 men, women and children had been brought to the prison during the three years of terror by the Khmer Rouge, and only seven got out alive.

The classrooms were very small, and each room was empty and clean except for a metal bed in the center of the floor. On one wall in each room was a poster-size black-and-white photograph showing a prisoner lying chained to the bed. In one photograph the chained man looked blackened and charred like an overcooked hotdog. He'd been electrocuted. In another room there was a collapsible army shovel lying next to to the bed, and the photo on the wall showed what seemed to be the same shovel lying in the same spot, and on the bed was a man who'd had his face scooped off his head. "Yes," our tour guide said, "the shovel was used to do this." He explained that the prisoners had been killed not by bullets or gas, but by farm tools such as shovels and picks, and so on.

In another building were hundreds, thousands, of photographs of the prisoners, all with numbers on their chest and their hands tied behind their back. Some other photos were of the guards who worked at the prison, and I realized that a lot of them were just kids, the same age as the kids who would have gone to school here—that the torturers and the killers had been children. It all seemed impossible, dark beyond comprehension. I started to get tunnel vision. I walked in tight circles around the room. I looked again at the photos, hoping that I'd been wrong in my assumption. I was not wrong. This happened.

Back in the bus all three of us were in favor of skipping the visit to the killing fields. We said we were tired and wanted to go back to the hotel. Our young Cambodian guide assured us that we could see the killing fields and be back at the hotel in an hour and a half. We had plenty of time. He was worried that we were not enjoying the tour, that things had somehow gone terribly wrong, and he was right.

On the way back to the hotel I asked him if he'd lost friends and family during the Pol Pot era, and he said, Yes, both of his parents and many of his relatives had died. Then he made a sweeping motion with his arm—the same motion made by the bartender at the FCC—

motioning out to the mass of traffic on Monivong Boulevard, saying, "Everybody lost members of their family, all of us."

I was sick at dinner, a formal dinner with coats and ties and invited guests from the Cambodian Ministry of Tourism—eighty-dollar bottles of wine, roasted duck, caviar. I had to excuse myself and go throw up in my wall-to-wall marble bathroom. I had something that made my bones ache like they'd been crushed; a high fever; a lot of sweating and shaking; deliriums while watching *Ghostbusters 2*. But the next morning I felt strong enough to return the motorcycle to Mr. Lucky, get my passport and fly with the other writers to Siem Riep. I was ready to start behaving in a more professional manner.

Siem Riep was a small town alongside a small river in the jungle—big trees, quiet streets, wooden huts elevated one floor off the ground and largely open to the air. The Grand Hotel d'Angkor—with five acres of gardens, a large swimming pool, tennis courts and a health spa—was even more lavish than Le Royal. It was a palace, a peach-colored castle with red ceramic tiles on the roof, originally designed and built in the 1930s using a mix of French and Buddhist architecture. It had been renovated over a period of three years by highly skilled craftsmen using the very finest materials, at a cost of several million dollars. It was both beautiful and repulsive. One night's lodging was more than a year's salary for the men who had restored it, and it was this type of colonial exploitation that had led to the early popularity of the Khmer Rouge's communistic ideology. Inside the hotel lobby were freshly cut flowers and servants in white jackets, standing at attention, waiting for the slightest sign to leap to action. Outside, beyond the gardens that served as a moat, were the dumbstruck zombies peddling broken bicycles, pushing wooden carts carrying thin green sticks for firewood, carrying dirt and adobe bricks, carrying naked babies with running noses and crusted eyelids. I told myself I needed to rest. I walked over to a bouquet of flowers in the foyer and stood there smelling the exotic scent, waiting to be checked into a room with clean sheets and *CNN Headline News*.

We had lunch with the provincial governor—a calm, older gentleman who spoke both English and French and was known to be an effective negotiator with the Khmer Rouge, most of whom, including Pol Pot himself, lived nearby in the highland regions along the border with Thailand.

"This area," he said, "is rich in Cambodian history, and we are very proud of our heritage. People come from all over the world to visit the Angkor temples, and we have gone to great lengths to ensure their safety. You may have read that an American couple was killed by the Khmer Rouge at Angkor in 1995, and that there was some shooting and fighting there during the military battles last summer, but, I can assure you, these problems are a thing of the past. I now have three hundred men guarding the area at all times."

I asked the governor if there were still land mines in the area, and he said the Angkor temples and the areas around them had been swept and were very safe, but that in his province, as a whole, an average of one person was blown up every week. "It's very sad," he said. "There are several international groups working every day, and then our country has its own division of de-miners, but there are many thousands still in the ground, perhaps more than can ever be recovered."

Very early the next morning we were taken to watch the sun rise over the most famous temple, Angkor Wat. This was a custom, almost a ritual, meant to bring a sense of awe and wonder to tourists' hearts. The place was huge, maybe 400 meters long and 400 meters wide, laid out in combinations of magical numbers and pure forms representing the fundamental metaphysical conceptions of the universe, constructed from red sandstone by a series of Hindu god-kings who ruled Cambodia from A.D. 800 to 1200. At the center of the temple was a shrine, six or seven stories tall, depicting Mt. Meru, the legendary home of Vishnu, the sustainer of the universe. There were cobra-fanned snakes called *nagas* flaring out from the peaks and corners, giving the appearance of flames. On the walls were finely chiseled reliefs showing Vishnu riding his winged chimera *garuda;*

Vishnu lying on top of a huge sacred *naga;* Vishnu floating in the sea of milk, while Brahma created the universe.

Our interpreter and guide was a young Cambodian man who'd been educated in East Germany and spoke English with a Cambodian/German/French accent. When the tour was over, he and I sat together on the stone wall of the long concourse leading into the temple, and I asked him why he'd chosen to go to school in East Germany. It seemed strange. He said that after the liberation of the country by the Vietnamese in 1978, many young Cambodians had been given scholarships there, and that he knew of some who were still in Germany out of fear that they would be persecuted if they returned.

"You've been to Toul Sleng Prison?" he asked. "Then you know that many of the murderers during the Pol Pot era were young, only children. The tourists who come here ask, 'How could this be?' but I will tell you that we had very much the brainwashing. The Pol Potees separated us from our parents, and they tell us that we are now the children of the organization. They give us the brainwashing, saying that the previous regime lived off the backs of the poor people, and that from now on all society would be equal. I would say that sixty to seventy percent of us lost our parents during that time, and there were those who confessed to the Pol Potees that our parents were high-level officials for the capitalists, because we believed they were the enemies of the organization. Some of us, not in the prison but in the work camps, even murdered our own parents, we were so much the brainwashing. The Pol Potees would come and ask us, 'Tell us the truth about your parents,' and those who wanted to be known as the hardest workers, who wanted to be promoted to be chief of ten or twenty other children, told the truth. I can tell you that when you are only fourteen years old and are the chief of twenty others, you feel very proud of your function. You know, we worked in the rice fields or building the dikes, and it was very nice, yes, very nice to be a chief. Then the Pol Potees would ask, 'Will you kill your parents?' and those who said they would were made even higher chiefs in charge of fifty children. And so now they do not want to come back and face their relatives."

"But how could they do that?" I asked.

"Oh, it was very easy," he said. "You have tied them at the hands and at the knees, down there, and they could not react at all. They kill them with the iron rod—the hoe and the shovel, or by placing the plastic bag over their heads, or by holding them under the water."

"And did you do this?" I asked, afraid of what he would say.

"No. I did not kill my parents."

"But were your parents killed?"

"Yes, I lost both of my parents. My father, you know, he was educated in Paris and served the capitalist regime as a high-level officer, a lieutenant colonel, working as an inspector for the Office of the Interior. When we were first taken to the camp he told the Pol Potees that he had been a taxicab driver, but then I was taken away from my parents to live with the other children and was given the brainwashing, and the Pol Potees asked me, 'Will you tell the truth about your parents?' So, because I very much wanted to be a hard worker, I told them the truth, and they made me chief. Every time in the meetings I was an example to show the other children—'Please, have a look at this one here.' But I did not know, I will tell you very honestly, I did not know that they would be killed. They told me they took my parents away to another camp, but three days later I saw the wife of our camp's leader wearing my mother's clothes, and I thought then that they had been killed."

"How do you feel about that?" I asked. "How do you live with the guilt?"

"You know, after the liberation we all saw what had happened, we saw for ourselves the many mass graves and the killing fields, and we were very angry. We wanted the revenge. I thought it was very terrible. But from year to year, we try to forget. We have one proverb—'The feeling of freedom is bigger than the feeling of revenge.' Now we are in a different philosophy. Before, when I was a child of fourteen in the concentration camp, I knew only for my stomach, and if I had some rice then everything was wonderful, you know, it was wonderful, because I did not know anything else. Now we know the modern world—we see motorcycles, we see the development that has come to our country, the rich investors, such as the director at the hotel, and this is what we want. We want these freedoms more than we want the revenge. It is very hard, and sometimes I think it is not fair that the investors come here because the labor is so cheap, but if we complain then the investors do not come. Our king, he says, 'Try to forgive. No more the war. We need to move on with the modern world. We need to cut the poverty.' And so this is what we do, but I think it will take a very long time."

In the evening of our last day in Cambodia I was told that the director had arrived at the hotel and would like to speak with me in his office. I thought perhaps I was in for a scolding, but the man received me warmly, saying he was sorry to hear about my illness and that he hoped I was feeling better. He was an American from the Midwest, in his late forties. His eyes were deeply bloodshot. His voice, however, was calm, even soothing, as if, after twelve years in the Far East, he had come to an enlightened state of quietude.

"I heard you had some questions for me," he said.

Questions? Did I have some questions? I had nothing but questions, none of which were answerable. For some reason I started babbling about free speech. I suppose I thought that what Cambodia needed was more democratic reforms—that both the communists and the capitalists had failed because of their repressions of individual liberties.

"I am not a politician," he said. "I am a businessman. I know that you have been talking to some people here, and are no doubt concerned about what you've been told, but, from my point of view, I think there is a real danger in coming into a country with a missionary zeal to make it into what you would like it to be. I've learned to listen and not to preach, to try to understand the environment from the sets of values that are established there. It's not that I am without principles. I have certain principles that I stick to no matter where I am. One of them is that whatever I do, I do it with my full passion and belief. Another is that I treat everyone fairly, regardless of their political party, and I've never had to waiver from these. We came here with a goal to accomplish something. These hotels were very much a part of the heritage of Cambodia, but they were incredibly worn down, so much so that the previous owners were considering tearing them down to the ground. But, when I saw them, I realized that the 'bones' were good, so to speak, and that the buildings wanted to come back. I promised three years ago that I would restore them to the highest possible standard, and we've done this; we've done this by creating a win-win situation, by creating an environment where our employees can take care of their family responsibilities, one in which they feel secure, and one in which they come to realize that this is a quest for knowledge. You know, the people here call me 'Papa,' because what we are really teaching them is how to have a future."

I had nothing to say to that. I had nothing left to say at all. I thanked the director for his time and for sponsoring my trip to Cambodia, and I left his office feeling worn out and numb. This condition lasted through the long plane ride back to the States and through a long period of weeks when I slept very little and spent the days afraid to leave my house.

I would like to say that all this has passed now, that I've recovered, and am a better person, overall, for having gone on the trip. But I don't really feel that this is true. The truth is that I don't feel much at all, and I am left remembering the words of Ed Fitzgerald—"I think you should tell people to come to Cambodia." The words echo in my mind like shouting in a cave. "Tell people to come to Cambodia . . . the more who see it, the better." And I know, somehow, that he is right.

1994

I'm always ready to go to Mexico to visit the Tarahumara. I have a map of the Barranca del Cobre (Copper Canyon) nearly memorized. I have an English-Tarahumara dictionary that I keep checking out from the university library. I'm ready if I can only get the money and if I can only get the time. But now, like a miracle, the Tarahumara have come to Salt Lake and are staying at my house. There are four of them, men between twenty-five and thirty-five years old. They're here to run in a hundred-mile ultra-marathon through the Wasatch Mountains.

Like always, I'm in the process of tearing the house apart, and there's no electricity because I'm redoing the service connection. We don't even have a service wire from the pole. But this is a good thing, I think, something that will make the Tarahumara feel at home. They don't have electricity. They don't even have outhouses.

Their manager is a backcountry tour guide from Tuscon, Arizona, and he tells me he's brought them here to raise money and get some media attention for their families back home, who are all starving to death. The Tarahumara are wearing their traditional clothing of long white shirts held at the waist by a belt and a pair of sandals cut from truck tires. They appear to be healthy enough, but I can't really tell. They're silent. They look mainly at the ground and move around my house as a unit, even to the bathroom. They look more frightened than malnourished.

We eat dinner outside where they seem more comfortable, and, afterward, I ask them (through a friend who speaks Spanish) if they've ever run down a deer. They say, no, the deer have disappeared and they don't know why. I ask them if they know other, older Tarahumara who did it, and they say yes, they know it was done, they've heard stories, and that the technique was to chase them for two to three days on end. They would sleep and then start tracking them down again in the morning. This is just as the ethnographic report described. Eventually the deer would stop and let them put a rope around its neck.

Two days later, three of the four Tarahumara finish first, second and fourth in the race. All run the hundred miles, up and down through the mountains, in less than twenty-one hours.

The editor of a well-known men's magazine called me on the phone and said he heard the radio story I'd done on Cambodia. He said that on his way to work he was thinking that his magazine hadn't had a war correspondent in a number of years and was wondering if I would like to do this. He said the idea was not that I would go cover big wars, as there were too many others already doing this, but that I would go to "really fucked-up places" that were not getting any media attention. He said he wanted me to start by going back to Cambodia.

cambodia, revisited

We fly into Anlong Veng on a military helicopter, a Russian Mi–8, running on most of its cylinders and carrying eighteen passengers, a chain saw, and 400 liters of gasoline in plastic cans that leak, filling the cabin with fumes. All of the passengers except for me and my translator, Narun, are soldiers in the Royal Cambodian armed forces, the army of military dictator Hun Sen. They are young, the infantrymen, and have machine guns: automatic Kalashnikovs from Russia and M16s made by Colt in Connecticut. The guns have a lot of miles on them. They are older than the boys who carry them, and seem to have more character, as if the guns were the passengers and the soldiers no more than tools and supplies. We fly with the side door open, looking out on the jungle below.

Anlong Veng is the former stronghold of the Khmer Rouge, former home to Brother Number One, Pol Pot, as well as Brothers Number Two, Four and Five, the leaders who orchestrated the genocide of two million people. The Khmer Rouge lived here in seclusion and secrecy as a militant, agrarian commune of twenty to thirty thousand people spread out over several hundred square miles. They grew rice and waged guerrilla warfare on the puppet government installed by the Vietnamese in 1979. They plowed their fields, and they made their own land mines and machine-gun bullets. The United States supported them as a "non-communist" faction, and they were given a seat in the United Nations, yet they abducted and tortured and killed tourists and foreign aid officials; they tortured and killed their own people for having had anything to do with anybody from the outside. Theirs was a pure vision of how a society should govern itself.

But it all fell apart on March 22 of this year, when 90 percent of the Khmer Rouge military defected to Hun Sen's army, essentially surrendering to the enemy. The villagers fled to refugee camps in the north and south; the four brothers and a small army of three hundred fled to the mountains along the border with Thailand.

So it seems that the Khmer Rouge has dissolved. Hun Sen appears to have consolidated his power, and, for the first time in anyone's recoverable memory, it seems as though Cambodians are not at war with themselves.

It's as if the entire country were waking up from a long, bad dream where it's unclear what is and is not possible, and all one can do is sit and wait and watch the world realign itself.

We land next to the hospital and, getting out from under the rotor, are passed by two soldiers carrying a third in a bloody hammock. He stepped on a land mine and lost a foot. They load him on board. Another soldier has a deer over his shoulder, quartered, its head and antlers coming up out of a rice bag. It goes on board. Four points.

I had imagined that Anlong Veng would be a town or a village, and it is, or was, I suppose, but it has no center or square, no post office, no bus depot, no temple, no police station, no lights on the street, no power lines in the air, no telephone cable. It is more a scattering of hardwood huts on stilts, surrounded by banana trees and gardens with pigs and chickens running around.

The one captivating feature of the town is an artificial lake two miles wide, and shallow, with a forest in the middle of it: fifty to sixty trees eighty to a hundred feet tall, all completely white and dead. At night, under a full moon, it would be the Lake of Doom. But in the full sunlight, the white trees in the blue and green lake are strangely beautiful. The sky has huge, billowing cumulus clouds a thousand feet tall—the jungle breathing, exploding in light.

We walk toward the lake to a group of huts occupied by soldiers standing around, listening to a field radio. I have Narun ask to speak with the commanding officer about getting permission to wander about freely. One of the men turns away from the radio and snaps, "The commanding officer isn't here. Go wherever you like, except not too far into the mountains as the Khmer Rouge will kill you. And don't go off the road as there are many land mines, which will also kill you."

So we walk back up to the road and sit in the shade at a picnic table. Farmers and their families come riding by on wooden carts with wooden wheels, pulled by oxen, carrying long planks of fresh, rough-cut hardwood. The wood, the oxen, the dirt on the road, even the Anlong Vengers themselves are the same color—deep reddish brown, ocher. Le Khmer Rouge.

They walk by and ride by, and some of them stop short, stunned when they see me. Three months ago, I would have been shot for sitting here. Three months ago, they would have been shot for looking at me sitting here. I ask Narun what they are looking at, and he says, "You. They're looking at you."

"Yeah, but why?"

And he says, "I don't know."

Perhaps, I think, they are aping me, mirroring my own expression. Perhaps I am the one who is stunned. And if I am stunned, it is for this reason: Nobody here looks like a killer. They look like dirt-poor peasants from the fourteenth century. Even the soldiers with guns seem tame and meek. I'm in the home of some of the most brutal murderers in history, and yet there's more tension of violence in the air in any shopping mall in America. I don't understand it. It must be part of the dream.

From where we sit, I can see an open-air assembly hall. Walking up to it, we see that it's now being used as a warehouse for captured rice and ammunition, with Captain Yat Soeun in charge. He is about fifty years old and wearing only a *krama* wrapped around his waist, his belly hanging over a couple of inches.

I ask him why the Khmer Rouge fell apart. Last year, he tells me, Pol Pot became suspicious of another high-ranking KR official, and he had him assassinated. He also had fourteen members of the man's family assassinated for good measure. This worried the other brothers, and last year they mutinied and arrested Pol Pot and put him on trial, right here in this assembly hall. They tried Pol Pot not for his crimes against humanity but for his crimes against the Khmer Rouge, for being a traitor to the struggle. The one-legged Ta Mok, Brother Number Four, was the leader of this group, and it is Ta Mok now who is the leader of the three hundred or so Khmer Rouge soldiers still hiding out in the mountains, willing to fight.

In the captain's opinion, Ta Mok was—and is—a very bad man. He had many people killed, and everybody was afraid of him. He controlled the profits from the trade in hardwoods to Thailand. He bought sawmills, restaurants, and hotels in Thailand and kept millions of dollars for himself and his family. This led the Khmer Rouge leaders to negotiate secretly with Hun Sen, hoping they could work a better deal through him.

I ask him how he knows these things, and he says this is what he was told by both defectors and captured Khmer Rouge soldiers whom they'd tortured. "We tied their hands and put them in those water barrels," he says pointing to three fifty-gallon oil drums just outside the building. He says this in the nicest way, as if they had invited the prisoners over for dinner.

As many as two million Cambodians died during the four years that the Khmer Rouge was in power. It was an agrarian revolution, and many who died were killed with farm tools—shovels, picks, digging sticks. Some were asphyxiated with plastic bags. Some were drowned. Many were ratted out or killed by their own children.

The political structure of the country is a pyramid of extortion, with Hun Sen on the top, various warlord gangsters (including the Khmer Rouge) just below, their cadres of assassins and thugs in the middle, and then the fishermen, farmers and foot soldiers (ninety percent of the population) on the bottom. For them, liberty is unknown. In Cambodia, it is useful to remember that actions do not necessarily have consequences. It is also useful to know that this is the way things have been in Cambodia for as long as anyone can remember.

Down at the crossroads, there's a shack that functions as a store, café and hangout. Narun and I order chicken noodle soup and sit in the shade. It's very hot and very humid, I'm dripping sweat; I'm overheating. I take out some sunscreen and rub it on my face and everybody stops talking and looks at me. "Protection," I say, pointing up at the sun. They nod, they look at the ground and the woman goes back to pounding with the meat cleaver.

The oldest man I've seen anywhere in Cambodia is sitting next to me in the shade. He's with his wife, who's about the same age. I ask the man how old he is, and his wife answers that he is seventy-three, the same age as Pol Pot when he died. The old man smiles. He has no teeth. It must be hard for him to talk. Or maybe he has lived so long because he has let his wife speak for him. They are farmers, and have been there since 1979. He was a soldier. I ask how their lives have changed since the defections in March, and the wife doesn't understand. I ask if her life, the way she lives, is different now, and she says, "I no longer have to make poison *punji* sticks to protect against the puppet government." She doesn't look at me or Narun when she speaks. I ask her what else is different and she says that's it. She used to have to make thousands of poison sticks every day to protect against the puppet government, and now she works in the fields and raises cows.

Narun and I rent bicycles, Chinese and completely beat to shit. The wheels rattle at the axles because there are no bearings. There are brake handles but there are no brakes; the frame is basically an agreement between sovereign parts, bound by lengths of wire found along the side of the road.

The biggest house by far in all of Anlong Veng is the home of one-legged Ta Mok. It sits on a rocky knob above the shore of the lake, looking out on the forest of dead trees. It is actually three houses together with a small courtyard in between. In the courtyard, there are four soldiers wearing boxer shorts and flip-flops, looking at something inside a chain-link dog cage. It's not a dog; it's a ten-foot python and a kitten. The kitten is soaking wet and lying collapsed, spread-eagle on top of the snake, unable to move and barely breathing. The python must have been squeezing it in the bowl of water, and then let it go. Clearly, there's a break in the action. We get a tour.

What can be said about the houses of the one-legged Ta Mok, Ta Mok the butcher? They are spacious without being grand. The largest room, closest to the lake, has one open wall facing the water, with a handrail to keep you from stepping off into the bushes. There's tile on the floor and big colorful murals across the other walls, idyllic scenes with elephants, deer and pheasants, and a waterfall—the good old days, a thousand years ago, back when the Khmer last kicked butt.

I stand at the veranda and look out at the lake with a soldier I assume to be an officer, perhaps a lieutenant, but it's hard to say, as his boxer shorts have no insignia. I'm looking at the trees and suddenly realize that a soldier is perched in one of them, sixty feet above the water. He must have swam out there and then somehow climbed the trunk that is smooth like ivory and three feet wide. He's got a machine gun, and I think he must be posted on guard duty, but the lieutenant says he's fishing. The trick is to shoot just in front of the head, so as not to demolish the flesh.

And then *Boom!* a big bomb goes off!

Okay, not a bomb but a hand grenade. Out across the lake there are three men up to their waist in the water. The lieutenant says that Ta Mok did not allow hand grenades for fishing, and so now the troops do it every day.

Boom!

Also in this big living room are two recent Khmer Rouge defectors. I ask them how old they are. One says he was born in the year of the chicken, the other in the year of the horse, which Narun figures to be eighteen and twenty, respectively. They say they've been soldiers since they were thirteen. They lived in groups of ten in the jungle under sheets of blue plastic and slept in hammocks without mosquito netting. They ate rice and salt, and burned fires to protect themselves from mosquitoes. They have no education; they never got paid. A lot of them got malaria; some died. Others stepped on land mines. They want to stop being soldiers. They want to be farmers now. They know I am not their enemy today, but what about tomorrow? And why would anyone ask questions like these?

The lieutenant lies down in a hammock, and I sit on a grass mat on the floor. He tosses me a pillow, and I lie down and take a break. He asks me how old I am, and I tell him, and he says he's the same age. I have three kids; he has three kids who live in Phnom Penh. I open a pack of cigarettes and take one, then toss it to him. We smoke and look at each other. I take a photo of him and then give him the camera and have him take a photo of me.

When we were boys, the same age as our kids are now, I was caddying at the country club and he was ducking and covering from 540,000 tons of bombs being dropped from American planes. I'm wondering if he doesn't hate America and Americans.

He says he doesn't, that he doesn't even hate the Khmer Rouge. They are good soldiers, very strong, and he's tired of fighting other Khmers, tired of fighting altogether.

There's a commotion from out in the courtyard. The snake is trying to get out of the cage. Everybody gets up and runs out there to stop it.

After dark, we go back to the meeting hall, where Captain Souen has made us dinner. Fish soup. Mud-fish soup. Hand-grenaded mud-fish soup. It tastes only like mud. I turn on my headlight and look at the soup, and it's reddish-brown, the same as the wood, the same as the oxen, the same as the road out of town. I choke down a few bites and then offer to buy some beer if any is to be had. Soon twelve cans of Angkor pilsner are on the table and four officers are sitting around helping to drink it. The smoke from our cigarettes goes down toward the ground like fog. Flying spiders, waning moon. The stories are of the horrors of the one-legged Ta Mok.

"They would come at night and kill the entire family."

Who would?

"Ta Mok's men."

Why would they kill them?

"Because they killed a rabbit, because they had five cigarettes, because they were seen walking down the road together, because they had been listening to the Voice of America. There are skulls down by the river. You can go see them."

"If a boy was caught fishing, the first time he would be reprimanded and scolded; the second time his hands would be tied and he would be dragged behind a car."

"It was forbidden to pick the mangoes in the trees along the road, but some boys were hungry and were up in a tree eating the mangoes, and Ta Mok came by in his car and got out and shouted up at the boys that they were traitors and betrayers of the struggle and that they should be shot."

And did he kill them?

"No, these he didn't kill, but he scared them."

Ta Mok scared the children, he frightened them, and this is somehow his most unforgivable offense.

The captain tells me I can take a shower before going to bed, which sounds great, but the shower turns out to consist of ladling water out of the oil drums by the assembly hall; the same drums in which the captain tortured his prisoners. I turn on my headlamp, and I look down into the water for ghosts. A woman sings a high-pitched Asian love song from a radio far out in the darkness. The water feels good when I pour it over my head.

I wake up inside the mosquito net and listen. The frogs and crickets have stopped. The air is still. I think I hear a very small motor, a dime-sized magneto spinning, running the safety light on the incubator lid. And then I remember that there is no incubator, that there is no motor, that the purring is just in my head.

The first lesson of the jungle is that forgetting is easy, that memory is quickly absorbed by the soil, that the trees and vines feed as much on darkness as they do on light. Two weeks before he died, Pol Pot said that he felt no remorse. In his first and last interview since losing control of the country in 1979, he said, "There's what we did wrong, and what we did right. The mistake is that we did some things against the people—by us and also by the enemy—but the other side, as I told you, is that without our struggle there would be no Cambodia right now. I came to carry out the struggle, not to kill people. Even now, and you can look at me, am I a savage person? My conscience is clear." Pol Pot lived just long enough to see his "struggle" dissolve and disappear. A couple of more weeks and even he could have forgotten all about it.

In the morning, we're down drinking instant coffee at the Don't Mok Me Crossroads Café, and there's a young man pacing up and down on the road in front of us, as though he has something to say.

He grew up in this area. He's twenty-three years old, named Bo. He was a Khmer Rouge soldier for six years, and he didn't like it. He said he had to live alone in the jungle and wasn't allowed to listen to the radio, but he did anyway. He listened to the Voice of America in Khmer from Bangkok, and when the United Nations officials came through town in 1992 to register people for the election, he hid on their truck as they were leaving. Now he's back, hoping to live here and work driving a truck, but he has no money and no job right at the moment.

"What would you buy if you had some money?" I ask.

"I would buy some rice to eat," he says.

"No, I mean if you had a lot of money, a hundred dollars."

He doesn't understand the question.

"I'm wondering what you want, or what you need. If you had a hundred or a thousand dollars right now, how would you use it?"

And he says, "That will never happen. I'll never have that much money. And if I did I would buy some rice to eat."

I give him some money, enough to buy breakfast.

Hun Sen, the military dictator, looks friendly enough in his pictures in the papers—young, intelligent, bespectacled. There he is accepting an honorary law degree from Iowa Wesleyan; there he is hugging his former enemy, the murderous Ke Pauk; there he is learning to play golf. He needs to relax in front of the ball.

But the man on the street will not say the words "Hun Sen" out loud. At most, he is referred to in a whisper as the second prime minister. This is because Hun Sen's opponents have a way of being found dead, missing eyes and tongues and hands. The United Nations Office of the High Commissioner for Human Rights has a list of more than one hundred dead since Hun Sen's coup in 1997. These one hundred do not include the seventeen who died from being hand-grenaded at an opposition political rally in March of 1997. No one was arrested. There will be no trial. The hand grenaders wore police uniforms.

In July, Hun Sen's party won the general election, and he was officially named prime minister, an outcome that was inevitable in the eyes of many. He had all the guns; he had the money; business was better than ever. Why would he have abdicated? Since the election, he has resorted to the kind of intimidation and brutality that marked his previous, unofficial tenure, as well as every Cambodian administration for the past twenty years.

In Cambodia, it's useful to remember that actions do not necessarily have consequences. In Cambodia, it's been this way for two thousand years. In Cambodia, it only looks like the civil war is over.

There are maybe twenty-five to thirty soldiers and civilians standing around, waiting for the helicopter in the shade of the hospital. All of them want to get on it, if it comes. One of them is the lieutenant from Ta Mok's house. He's in uniform and carrying a full knapsack. I don't need to ask him—I know he's got a leave, and he's going home to see his wife and kids.

Narun tells me that there are too many people waiting, that some of them, maybe even us, will not get on the helicopter. I say that perhaps I can pay the pilot something. Narun thinks this might be a good idea. And then I hear it. Narun says it's a chain saw, but we wait and it's a helicopter, the same one that brought us in. We all walk over to where it lands and stand there while they unload gasoline and some medical supplies from Doctors Without Borders. And then the man in the door motions for Narun and me to get in.

They load people and supplies, the pilot grumbling about this being a military helicopter and he doesn't know why he's flying civilians. They let some soldiers on. They stop boarding, they argue and fight a bit. Two more board, and that's it. I look around and count twenty-five passengers. The lieutenant didn't make it. I look out the door and he's standing there, looking at me—the same stunned look that I didn't understand yesterday, but now I do. It's the look that comes from seeing what might have been, where you want to remember but already you've forgotten. He's stuck in Anlong Veng, and he's not dreaming. The door closes, the chopper bucks and levitates over the jungle, and I am out of there.

1996

As an experiment of my own I have convinced a few friends and a band to come out to Puddle Valley and try to lure the antelope into our camp by playing loud music day and night.

I have read that the Goshute Indians, the indigenous people of the Great Salt Lake Desert, could charm antelope by constructing a semimagical ring around them. They would make a large circle, 200 yards in diameter, marked by six mounds built from sticks and bushes. Then they would pound a drum and dance, and, after a period of five days, the antelope would come inside the ring and then run in circles, convinced that they were trapped. Antelope have a thing with circles—perhaps because they can see in nearly 360 degrees.

We camp in the area where I've most often seen the lone male. We have a generator and big speakers, and we build six twenty-foot towers from willow branches. Then we tie long thin flags to the towers so that they blow in the wind and you can see them from a distance.

But there are no antelope around. It's the only time I've been out here and not seen the lone male. I think everybody is wondering if maybe I'm just making all this up, but I know that there are antelope out there, and that they are listening and looking and that they will remember us the next time.

kashmir

Jesus died in Kashmir. You can see his tomb and his footprints in Srinagar, the capital city. He was ten feet tall and would have worn size thirty shoes. Also, he was extremely flat-footed. The story is that he spent the "lost years" of his youth wandering in the Himalayas and, through tantric methods he learned from Buddhist monks, was able to fake his death on the cross by stopping his heart and lungs. Then they lowered his body and put it in a cave, and after three days he got up and said, "So, okay then," and walked back to Kashmir, the most beautiful place on earth, with his best friend, Thomas, and his girlfriend, Mary.

The story is that Kashmir has a long history of saints, holy men, poets, and philosophers who were drawn to the mountains and valleys for their beauty—snow in the winter (but not too much and not too cold), green and fertile in the summer, falls like New England, and spring floods from the canyons of the central Himalayas. No less than the Buddha himself is said to have remarked that Kashmir is the best land for meditation and leading a religious life.

But out on the street, just outside the tomb of the giant Jesus, you can't walk fifty yards in any direction without passing a sandbag bunker manned by Indian Security Forces pointing machine guns at passersby. Out on the street, there are holes in the asphalt made by hand grenades. There are burned buildings, empty buildings, and when the sun goes down, the streets themselves are completely deserted except for roving packs of homeless mongrel dogs. No one dares to venture out, and yet they are not even safe inside behind locked doors, as every night six to twelve people are machine gunned dead in their homes. In the past nine years, fifty thousand Kashmiris have been killed.

This would seem ironic, but a quick read of the history shows that while Kashmir has been, and perhaps still is, the spiritual heart of the Indian subcontinent, it has also always been contested territory. It is not only beautiful and rich in agriculture and water resources, it is centrally located on the trade routes of the southern Himalayas. Kashmir is the passage to India—as well as to China, the Middle East, and Europe. And over the past two thousand years, as Brahmins and Buddhists and Muslims prayed and prayed all day, Kashmir has been ruled by no less than twenty-one dynasties that invaded from all directions of the Asian continent—raping, plundering and subjugating those who would otherwise be lost in prayer.

And while it is true that the Kashmiri takes pride in his deep intellectual and spiritual roots, it is also true that he has, over the centuries of subjugation, developed a chameleon-like character and is willing to stoop to sychophancy and servility. So today you are more likely to hear a sob story from a Kashmiri than a pastoral poem. He will more likely try to hustle and con you than engage in a philosophical debate. "Kashmir is the most beautiful place in the world, is it not?" he will ask you. "Yes," you will want to respond, "Kashmir is the most beautiful place in the world, but there are many places just as beautiful, and few, if any, are as sad."

The current dispute over Kashmir has been going on since the day India and Pakistan were born. It started this way: In 1947, the British admitted that India was more trouble than it was worth and decided to pull out as quickly as possible. Gandhi wanted the entire subcontinent of 562 princely states and 200 languages to be one united democracy, but the Muslims wanted their own state, with their own government, the kind where Allah is in charge. The British, for reasons that probably had as much to do with expediency as ethics, opted for the partition and quit the subcontinent, declaring that any predominantly Muslim state that was contiguous with Pakistan should become part of Pakistan. By this design, Kashmir should have gone to Pakistan, but it didn't turn out that way. Pakistan sent troops to invade Kashmir, and they got within four miles of Srinagar before India sent a brigade to beat them back.

In 1948, the United Nations Security Council passed a resolution stating that the Kashmiris should be given the right to determine whether to become a part of India or Pakistan, but, fifty years and four wars later, the Kashmiri people have yet to vote on the issue. Today, Pakistan has one-third of Kashmir, India has two-thirds, and inbetween is a blurred area known as the Line of Control, where the two armies have engaged in almost continual skirmishing, even far up in the Himalayas at 20,000 feet above sea level on the Siachen Glacier.

In 1988, the border dispute turned into a civil war, as thousands of Kashmiri youths went to Pakistan and Afghanistan for guns and training in guerrilla warfare and then came back to Srinagar, the capital city, demanding the right to self-determination. They began blowing up police stations, abducting and assassinating government officials, and burning the homes of the Hindus, forcing 240,000 of them to flee and seek refuge in Jammu or farther south into the rest of India. In the beginning, the Kashmiri people supported the militants by giving them food and shelter and money, and the militants lived in and around Srinagar, walking the streets with their weapons, and bragging about their exploits.

India responded by sending 250,000 troops to occupy Kashmir, outnumbering the militants by fifty to one. They killed many of the leaders and imprisoned many more. They imposed curfews and searched homes and whole neighborhoods, arresting and killing militants, arresting and killing anyone who might have helped the militants, raping some of the women, burning homes to the ground.

By 1992, most Kashmiri people had stopped giving the militants food and shelter and money, but the militants took it from them anyway, as they also had a license to kill: they were fighting a jihad, and anyone who opposed the jihad was an enemy of Allah. And so the Kashmiri people were caught between two impossible choices—

either help the militants and suffer at the hands of the Indian Security Forces, or cooperate with Security Forces and suffer at the hands of the militants. The result has been that now a Kashmiri cannot safely trust his own brother, perhaps not even his own son. The fabric of their culture is dissolving in fear.

So, O.K. then. Jesus, at age thirty-three, walked back to Kashmir, the most beautiful place in the world. He was ten feet tall, and the Kashmiris called him Isa Sahib. He was glad to be back in the mountains, and glad that Thomas and Mary had come with him. He died at age 125, and is buried in a tomb in Srinagar.

The story is that Srinagar used to be a happy place, a happening place, with bars and thousands of tourists, pilgrims looking for gurus, and mountain climbers. Tourism was Kashmir's number-one industry, and business was good. My driver, Majid, describes it this way: "Every night we bringing home the chickens. Every night we bringing home the vegetables. We making the wife. We making the children. Life is good. But then everywhere there is fighting, and the tourist is no more coming."

Majid drives me around Srinagar, a mud-web city with cave-like shops selling sheep ankles, collected nuts and bolts, Indian music on cassette. There are people yelling in five languages; there is Indian music blaring out of a bad loudspeaker; there are cows and goats and chickens and horses in the road, cars and trucks pouring out black smoke and continually honking, honking, honking.

Majid shows me a neighborhood in the old part of the city that looks like Dresden. There are shops on the street, but they are all closed down. Two days ago, a hand grenade was thrown by militants at the security force bunker just across from the shops, and it bounced off and went off in the road. I look at the scatter print in the asphalt where it exploded, and it's like you would draw a meteorite exploding in space. No one was killed, but Indian Security Forces went from house to house, yelling and screaming, pointing their guns and beating up the Kashmiri men, kicking them in the face and smashing their bones with the butts of their guns. They show me their bruises. They say an eighty-year-old man was put in the hospital. They're sad and scared, depressed in a terrorized sort of way. But, for these people, having a bomb explode outside their shops and then getting beat up in their homes is not such a big deal. They could have been killed, after all, and they weren't, and maybe this is a good thing. It's hard to be sure.

Majid takes me to the homes of some of the political opposition leaders. All are fundamentalist Muslims, and each tells me they are fighting for the right to self-determination, like America with the British two hundred years ago. Majid takes me to see Yasin Malik in jail. He's is one of the four original insurgents, each of them teenagers at the time, who went to Pakistan for training and weapons, and came back to Srinagar and convinced thousands of other youths to follow them. Malik, now thirty-two, is the chairman of the Jammu and Kashmir Liberation Front (one of many Muslim-separatist organizations). More than any other leader, he seems to be respected, even trusted, among the Kashmiris.

I ask to go to Malik's cell, but the police insist on bringing him to the jail-keepers' office to meet me. He slumps on a bench with his back against the wall like he has no strength to sit up. He glares at me, what do I want? I tell him I'd heard that he had a bad heart, and I apologize for making him walk from his cell. He tells me that he's getting released in the afternoon, and that I should come by and see him at his home.

We buy a chocolate cake for Yasin's family, and find their home in the old part of the city. Yasin sits on the floor, leaning against the wall, and I ask him what happened to his heart. He says he got blood poisoning one of the first times he was in jail, and then later he had a heart transplant, also while he was in jail. He seems pretty weak. I ask him if he ever looks back with regret on his decision to take up the struggle. "There is no question of regret," he says. "We want to live with respect, honor and dignity. If there is no dignity, no respect, no honor, then what for the life? It has no meaning. So this movement will continue."

A lot of people, especially the Indian officers, are very much of the opinion that the militancy is manned by foreigners from Pakistan and Afghanistan and Saudi Arabia. Is this true?

"There is some percentage of people who came from different countries," he says. "But it is not true the movement is dominated by them. Look, in 1991 and 1992 the militants used to walk freely on the road. Now the situation has changed. The government of India makes targets of the family members of the militants. They are brutally killed, their houses blasted. Three months back in Jatrakund, there is one militant named Badrukand. The local brigadier of the army called his father into headquarters and told him to bring his son. The poor father told him, 'I do not know the whereabouts of my son. He has made the decision to not have contact with me. When I don't have any kind of contact with him, how can I produce him?' The brigadier gave him four days. In four days, he again was called and asked why he did not bring his son. The father told him, 'I already told you I have no contact.' The brigadier said, 'I give you twenty-four hours.' Twenty-four hours expired. The whole family was sleeping. They planted explosives in the house, the whole house was blown up and seven members of the family died. This is the situation here. The Kashmiri does not want to be identified as a militant because he knows what will happen to my family members."

I tell Malik that the Indian officers believe that the militants are weak, that they can never defeat the 600,000 troops now occupying Kashmir and that the militants are simply trying to stir up international attention.

"Yes, that is their version," he says. "They suffer from the arrogance of power. They believe in might. They are using their might on the innocent people of Kashmir. But we will continue. From the last eight years, they could not break the will of the people, and I don't think in the future they will break the will of the people. They are using force and through force they are here, otherwise they have no place on the soil of Kashmir."

Majid, my driver, belongs to a somewhat secretive political party whose name he translates as meaning "Sit-on-the-Porch Militants." He says they are nonviolent and want jobs more than self-determination. "Everyone working," he says. "Everyone sitting on porch with his family." But, he says, the party has not yet openly declared itself, and that it might be better all around if I didn't mention its name or ask anyone else about it.

The roads and traffic in Kashmir are wild systems, and Majid is a good driver. He folds his rearview mirror in against the door in order to get four more inches of passing space—space he actually uses, many times, in many creative ways. There are no stop signs or traffic signals and the traffic is literally bumper-to-bumper and door-to-door even at twenty and forty miles an hour, like a roller coaster with two-way traffic and one track.

But much worse than the cramped conditions is the exhaust from the rusted engines. Trucks and cars blow out black clouds of smoke, and the air on any road in Kashmir could not be any closer to unbreatheable. I am continually checking my instinctive flee mechanism, fighting back claustrophobia and the resulting desperation. Fifty thousand Kashmiris have died by violent means since the insurgency began in 1989, but I wouldn't be surprised if many more have died prematurely due to lung diseases.

We drive out of Srinagar and northwest down the Valley of Kashmir. I've heard that the valley was once covered by a lake 150 miles long and 40 miles wide and that the topsoil here is one mile deep. There are farms everywhere and it's harvest time. There are apples and roasted corn for sale along the road. Women are carrying big aluminum pots of hot tea, balanced perfectly on their heads, out to the workers in the fields—the kind of scene where you'd never know there was a civil war going on. The men in the fields with scythes could be militants who have their machine guns hidden nearby, the women carrying tea could be highly skilled in the manufacture of bombs. The battles have become more like terrorist acts, the insurgents disappearing into the landscape, and the Indian forces, like the Americans in Vietnam, are left believing that anyone and everyone is the enemy.

I have bought all fifty back issues of the *Kashmir Monitor*, a new Srinagar daily—four pages for one rupee. "The headlines are always somewhere between breathtaking and unbelievable: "19 Muslims Gunned Down in Cold Blood in Poonch Village"; "India and Pakistan Trade Artillery Fire, Charges—'It's All Out War on the LoC'"; "Infiltration Bid Failed, 16 more Lives Lost." The photos are of 160mm Bafore guns firing on the line of control, bodies lined up to be buried, boys running on the street from soldiers with gas and guns. From reading the papers it would seem that the entire country is either under, or on, fire.

On every bridge we cross, Majid says, "This bridge bombed by the militants, the army rebuilds it." At every community and scattering of houses he tells a tale of woe: "Here the militants put the bomb in the road, they they do not tell the local people. The bomb explodes, killing a Security Forces truck. The soldiers burn the houses and kill three men in the village, even though they did not know. And if they did know, if they tell the Security Forces, they are killed, their homes are burned by the militants. It is the poor people who suffer, always it is the same."

We drive through Baramulla, a town forty miles west of Srinagar, known as a hotbed of insurgency, and stop outside the compound of the district commissioner. The compound is a square enclosure, a dirt courtyard, the size of a city block, flanked by offices that seem to have the false facades of a Hollywood western. One building has a sign on the front that says "Court" and another that says "Sub-Court." There are prisoners, young men, with chains on their ankles and wrists, which the police hold like dog leashes. Wives and fathers and brothers are on the perimeter sitting, waiting, some for days, exhausted from unending worry for their family members who have been arrested without charge and will be jailed without release until they are tortured and confess to everything including their hatred for life itself, or are relieved of its burden forever.

A man in an oversized suit is pacing the courtyard, lost in thought. I say, "Excuse me, sir." He looks up, too tired to be surprised, and motions for me to follow him through a door and back to a small dark office where he offers me a seat at his desk. "Would you have some tea?"

He's a lawyer for the militants who have been arrested, of which there were no less than 2,000 in the Baramulla jails alone. He is completely intense, wound as tightly as a magneto coil. None of his clients have been or will be charged—they are simply held, and some have disappeared. He pleads for their innocence, saying that they have been forced to take up the guns in self-defense.

"You are here because of the nuclear explosions, which have drawn the attention of the international community, and are a threat to the peace, not only for the entire subcontinent, but for the entire world," he says. "But we, the Kashmiri people, are fighting to be allowed the right to self-determination. We are being burned for offenses we have not committed, we are being jailed and killed, our sisters and mothers raped many times for the offense they have not committed."

He looks like he is going to spontaneously combust, and I'm sorry to have taken him away from his pacing, where he seemed only very agitated. "You can go to the jail and see for yourself," he says.

The jail. I go there, and the officer in charge, in mirrored sunglasses, just laughs at me. Everyone in the office, including the secretaries, laughs at me. We leave Baramulla. I tell Majid to drive quickly.

We go north into the countryside, sixty miles to Kupwara, a town in a broad river valley surrounded by mountains, very near the line of control. Some of the Kashmiri militants, after being trained in camps in Pakistan and Afghanistan, come up the Kupwara Valley and cross back into Kashmir. Two weeks earlier, a fierce two-day battle took place here between militants and Security Forces. An Indian captain, eleven of his men, and more than two dozen militants were killed.

I get out at the checkpoint and a young captain—Vinot—asks "Why are you here?" I tell him I want to talk to people about how the militants come through here. I want to know how many of them are actually Kashmiris. "They come through all over this area, and we shoot them and take their weapons," he says. "Only thirty percent of them are Kashmiris, the others are from Pakistan and Afghanistan, a few from Sudan. They come across and we catch them and shoot them. What else would you like to know?" The captain comes from Rajasthan, but his manner is British. He tells me that I am now under his jurisdiction, and it is only through the goodness of his heart that he will let us into the town. "Talk to anyone. There are no problems in Kupwara. But don't go beyond the town, do not cross the river, as it is very dangerous there."

We get back in the car and go down into the central market, but it's teeming with soldiers. I suggest going to the edge of town, into the fields to talk with people, and Manzoor, my twenty-year-old translator, goes cold and stiff in his seat. The captain had told Manzoor that if he took me out of the market he would come find us and shoot him—not at all very British.

So we go out in the fields and try to talk to some men on a tea break, but they're really nervous. They can't believe I'm standing there asking them questions. I tell them thanks and start taking pictures of people harvesting what looks like wheat but is actually rice. They cut the tall stalks with small scythes and then tie them into bundles, which are then carried by women, balanced perfectly on their heads, to the road.

While I'm taking pictures a young man comes up and sits beside me. The way he tells the story, the incident two weeks ago wasn't a battle between militants and Security Forces but a slaughter of villagers in the nearby village of Jaggarapora—nineteen men, all civilians, one of whom was between eighty and ninety years old. The Security Forces burned the village and shelled the fields, destroying the crops. I ask the young man if this was the first time this had happened, and he says, "No, it has happened many times. Many people have died."

Driving back through town we're stopped by whistling soldiers and Captain Vinot is called on the radio. He comes speeding up in his jeep and screeches to a halt. He's upset.

"Where did you go?" he says.

Just into the fields.

"And who did you talk to?"

"I was mainly taking photographs," I say. "The people didn't seem to want to talk. They seemed afraid."

Manzoor is about ready to pee in his pants.

"And what did they say?"

"Just what you already told me—that people are killed every day."

He calms down and asks me about Bill Clinton. I make up a story about Clinton and Lewinsky in the Oval Office, one involving beastiality. Vinot is shocked. He asks if this is true. I tell him that I heard it as inside information, and that soon everyone will know about it. He lets us go.

It gets dark, and Majid sticks in some Indian music. We're most of the way back to Srinagar when Manzoor tells me how Vinot had threatened him. I ask him why he didn't tell me when it happened, and he doesn't answer. He was too frightened, I suppose. I start wondering about Vinot. He could have found the field and arrested everyone. He could torture them. He could kill them. But he won't. It just doesn't seem possible.

We sleep on Manzoor's father's houseboat, and in the morning we head east along a highway through the Himalayas. The road eventually reaches Leh, in Ladakh, but we're going about half that distance, to visit an area on the line of control where the level of militancy is low, but Indian and Pakistani artillery units are fighting each other. The bombing has been going on since July, two months ago, when the snow melted enough for the highway to open. The Pakistanis are positioned high up in the mountains, sending shells from out of the clouds, down into Indian Kashmir. Thousands had landed on the town of Kargil, killing six people, and another six fell on the road coming into town.

The shops in Kargil are closed. Yesterday Pakistan shelled the town in three barrages—morning, noon and night. Now the Indian cannons are firing, one shot every half-hour, and then two in a couple of minutes, lobbing one-hundred-millimeter shells back over the mountains . . . The only way to know would be to have someone on the ridgelines, at sixteen thousand feet, looking down the other side. Somewhere over there is a town just like Kargil, with its shops all closed.

We zigzag up the side of a mountain, along terraced fields, through apricot and almond orchards, to a hamlet called Goma. Some of the men show us where a young mother was killed, a piece of shrapnel piercing her heart as she ran out to rescue her baby boy. One man tells me that nearly everyone in the village has left, and that there will not be enough food this winter. He says they're scared—their homes were being hit, the roof of their school had a bomb go right through it.

I ask him if he understands why India and Pakistan are shelling each other, and he says no, he does not understand it. I ask the other men, and they say they do not understand it either. They don't know why the armies are shelling back and forth, killing Kashmiris on both sides. Then one of the men asks me to tell people that the United States needs to stop the shelling. And they all looked at me, six or seven men, studying my face as if there might be some hope to be found there.

In the evening I end up in a small press conference with two Kashmiri photo journalists from Srinagar. One shoots stills for Agence France Press and the *Kashmir Daily*, the other does video for the World News Service. Colonel Nair, the commanding officer in the Kargil area, begins the interview by saying there will be no interview. "None of you have written permission from office of press relations, and so I am of course prevented from answering any of your questions. It is simply a matter of protocol."

He turns to the the videographer and says, "Where is the decoder you promised me? When I get my decoder you will get your inter-view."

Then he turns to me and says, "We have no sports without cable.

I'm missing the Davis Cup. And what is the condition of your President Clinton?"

I say, "It seems he will have to say he is sorry and beg for Christian forgiveness."

"And will this work?"

"No, probably not, as America is not really a Christian country."

"Why are you here?" he asks me.

I tell him I want to know why India and Pakistan are killing civilians. He says, "There are plenty of other insurgencies to cover, no less than six going on in other parts of India. And then there are the Basques in Europe. Surely we don't hear enough about the Basques. Why don't you report on them?"

He has a way of talking all the time but saying nothing. He seems to be enjoying himself. While he talks I look at the huge topographic map under glass on his desktop. It makes the colonel nervous to see me studying it. "Let me ask you a theoretical question," I say. "Let's suppose that one army has a higher and, therefore, superior artillery position and is firing at will down on another army as well as the surrounding village of farmers. But let's also assume that the second army has helicopters and fighter jets. Let's say it has a lot of them. Why wouldn't the general of that army take out the artillery from the air?"

The colonel looks at me, almost smiles and says, "This is not a war we are fighting here. This is only friendly fire."

So Jesus left the cave and walked back to the Himalayas where he had been so happy as a young man. He was glad to be back in the mountains, and he was glad Thomas and Mary had come with him. But eventually Thomas and Mary fell in love with each other and moved away to live in Goa on the coast. Jesus stayed in Kashmir and taught the people to fly-fish with pine needles. I tell Majid that the story, according to the colonel, is that all the shelling is just friendly fire, and we shouldn't worry. Majid laughs all the way back to our hotel, and is still laughing the next morning at 3:30 as we drive out of town with our lights turned off so as not to be a target. We are creeping along, trying to see the winding road in the night, catching glimpses of the river nearly five hundred feet straight down. Majid is laughing and singing, so happy to be exposed to the friendly fire, the brisk mountain air. So good to be a Kashmiri. I tell Majid that he is a madman, a wild man, and he says, "Yes, it is true!" and sticks in a cassette of Indian tabla music, a woman singing about the ocean.

I ask Majid what he thinks will happen to Kashmir, and he says he doesn't know, that only God knows. "God knows everything."

I ask him, Why, if God knows everything and controls everything, is he punishing the Kashmiris? "Only God knows these things," he says, turning down the music. "Nine years we have suffered very much, many people have been killed by the gun. For us nine years is a long time, but nine years for God is nothing. It is a very small thing."

We drive back into Srinagar through the old part of town. The Muslims are praying, the moaning pleas coming out of loudspeakers from every direction. We honk and weave through the mud-web of narrow alleys—everyone in town with a headache and a frown from being scared shitless for years. All wandering. All waiting for God to listen to their prayers and do something to help them.

Jesus died in Kashmir. He was one hundred and twenty-five years old and extremely flat-footed, and it just hurt too much to walk around anymore. One day he sat down on the side of the road next to an old man roasting ears of corn over a fire and said, "So, O.K. then," and left his ten-foot body behind. The story is that he is coming back. The story is that the governments of India and Pakistan are ready to solve the Kashmir dispute. They are having meetings, they are talking, trying not to threaten each other with nuclear annihilation. The story is that things are returning to normal in Kashmir, and that there will be peace again in the valley, the most beautiful place in the world.

1997 the Seri

After two years of passing paper back and forth with the IRS I have formed a nonprofit corporation to raise money to produce a documentary movie about running down antelope. To begin, we travel to the Sea of Cortez to tape interviews with the Seri Indians, who are said to be able to run down deer. I've asked my friend Creighton King to come along. Also I've invited a cameraman/interpreter, Fabian, an Indian from Ecuador studying filmmaking at the University of Utah.

Creighton is the best runner I know. He's forty-three years old and probably past his prime, but a decade or two ago he was a virtual wonder of speed and endurance in the mountains. For instance, he once ran to the top of the Grand Teton and back down in less than four hours. He also ran back and forth across the Grand Canyon—from the south rim down to the river and up to the north rim and back, a distance of forty-two miles with more than 22,000 feet of elevation loss and gain—in less than eight hours. If the Seri still chase deer, then perhaps Creighton can run and actually keep up with them. Then we will have firsthand experience and an actual record of the thing.

It's a thousand-mile drive through Arizona and the Mexican state of Sonora, through Hermosillo and then west to Kino Bay, a small tourist town on the coast, where we turn north and drive up a thirty-mile dirt road to Punta Chueca, a small village built on a strip of sand between the desert and the sea. Two hundred Seri live here in cinder block homes painted white and baby blue, with the doors and windows either open or missing altogether, and the yards separated by fences made from branches and sticks and worn-out fishnets. It's a fishing village, but there's no harbor and only a few boats are anchored just off the beach. They, too, are painted white and baby blue and are all the same, long and heavy fiberglass skiffs powered by a seventy-five-horsepower outboard motor. They're like pickup trucks in the water.

We meet Ernesto Molina, a Seri fisherman and tourist guide. He's fifty years old and speaks excellent Spanish, very calm and soft spoken, a graduate of a college in Prescott, Arizona. It turns out he is also the grandson of Francisco Molina, who was the guide for Charles Sheldon, an American hunter who visited the Seri in 1921. I've brought a book containing Sheldon's account, and Ernesto shows me the photos of his grandfather. He knows the passages where Sheldon writes about Francisco's amazing knowledge and strength as a hunter.

We sit with Ernesto on the beach, and he tells us that yes, it's true, the Seris at one time, before they had rifles, would run after deer until they dropped from exhaustion.

"How would they prepare for this?" Creighton asks.

"It was a common practice," Ernesto says, "to prepare young men in the winter by not allowing them to come near the fire, to keep them away so that the heat would not enter their stomachs, and, in this way, develop their strength and stamina. And then, in July, the young hunter would be given a special drink of two or three types of plants"—he wouldn't say which ones, but it was a power food of some kind to give him strength and fortitude—"and then he would go off and track the deer alone. Finding the deer, he would pursue it, running after it in heats. In the first, the deer would be frightened and run very quickly. It took great skill and knowledge to follow it, never losing sight of the animal, and making sure he was still following the same one. Eventually the hunter would catch up with the deer and it would run again, this time more slowly and less of a distance, only two or three kilometers. Again, the hunter must make sure that he did not lose sight of it and that it was the same deer."

"Yes," I say, "we had that problem with pronghorns."

"The deer would stop again to rest," Ernesto continues, "and again the hunter would catch up with it. This time, the third time, the deer would realize that the hunter was stronger, and the deer would become disoriented, because after all, although the deer is very smart, it doesn't have the intelligence of a human being. The deer would become completely fatigued, beaten down, and sometimes it would fall and not get up. Sometimes the hunter would kill it with a rock. This was the method, the technique that was used."

"Have you ever hunted this way?" Creighton asks.

"No," he says. "My grandfather Francisco could do it, but when Francisco died the technique died with him."

"Are you sure that this was actually done?" I ask.

"Both my grandfather and father told me about this," he says. "They were both great hunters and knew the ways of the deer. But now there are much fewer deer, and then the government does not even allow them to be hunted. There are two elders here in the village, the Montano brothers, and they also know about the technique, as their father also could do it. We can talk to them tomorrow if you'd like."

We sleep on the beach with the sound of small waves, somewhat dazed and shocked by the fact that you can drive a thousand miles and come to the edge of the earth.

In the morning we interview both Cuy and Chewy Montano. They're about sixty-four and seventy years old, but they don't know for sure as neither one can remember the month or year they were born. They speak Seri, which is translated by Cuy's son. Cuy tells us that the hunter would chase the deer three or four times, and that it would take about two or two and a half hours before the deer would collapse. Chewy says that the hunter would sometimes use the head of a deer, holding it like a mask, imitating very closely the movements and behavior of a deer, which would make the prey curious, drawing it closer and closer, until they could somehow jump on it or barrage it with rocks.

Creighton asks them if there are any runners in the village who would like to try this again, and they say no, that they no longer run, that everything has changed. I ask Chewy if it is better now.

"No, not at all," he says. "It was better before. We used to do everything as a family. The whole community was a family. We shared everything and cooperated, but now there is a lot of arguing and bickering, every man for himself."

We drove home kind of sad, as it seemed like there were no more people alive on the planet who hunt without weapons.

chiapas

A Rough Beginning

I saw her first from behind, slipping away in a crowd in San Cristobal de las Casas. We were on the street outside the conference center where Zapatista leaders were meeting with legislators from the Mexican government. After two years of silence, the Zapatistas had come out of the jungle under escort of the Red Cross. They left their machine guns at home, but kept their black balaclava ski masks and green fatigues and looked like professional wrestlers next to the gray-haired legislators in sport coats and authentic Indian ponchos. There were a couple of hundred people standing around outside waiting to see what would happen. I was walking along, not looking where I was going and sort of ran into her, just brushed her. "*Cuidado*," she said, be careful, and just kept going. I turned and saw her. She was tall and willowy, long blond hair, lissome. And gone.

I'd been in Chiapas for four days and things were going poorly. I'd been taken into the jungle by a group of Mexican journalists and abandoned, only to make my way back to San Cristobal where I'd been robbed, losing a bag with my passport, $700 in cash, my camera and a notebook. I needed some help—someone who could function as an interpreter and a guide, but the conference event had attracted a large number of international television journalists willing to pay $150 a day for such services, which was simply beyond my budget, especially after losing a large chunk of my expense money. I thought that the young woman, who walked like an American, might be a good bet. I ran and caught up with her. I introduced myself and asked if she knew what was happening inside the conference.

"It's over, at least for today," she said. "It lasted only forty-five minutes. The Zapatista leaders accused the Mexican legislators of being racists, no better than the conquistadores. They said that their hotel here in town is cold and dirty, that they have no hot water and the toilets are broken, and that there's no security, no armed guards, to protect them. They're really pissed off. They pounded the table and walked out."

"But the two sides are enemies, aren't they?" I asked. "The Zapatistas declared war on the Mexican government. Why should the legislators put them up in a good hotel?" She looked at me like I was some kind of asshole. I asked if she had a few minutes, maybe enough time to sit down and have some coffee and talk.

She was twenty-three years old and didn't want me to use her real name, so I'll call her Sarah and say she was from Oregon, which is close enough to her real home. She'd been in Chiapas for four months as an international observer monitoring human rights abuses, living in La Realidad, the same village where I'd been abandoned by the journalists. She said there were nine or ten other observers in the village, mostly from Europe and Mexico City, and that they stayed there in order to prevent the Mexican army from killing the inhabitants or chasing them off the land.

"It's a very complex situation," she said. "How long are you going to be here?"

"About ten days."

"Ten days? You'll never figure it out in ten days. It's pretty arrogant and stupid to even think you could get close to it in that much time."

"I'm not writing a dissertation," I said. "It's a short column on really fucked-up places for a men's magazine."

"A men's magazine with tits on the cover? Some blood and guts between advertisements for three-thousand-dollar suits and cologne? There are a lot of those magazines now and they make me sick."

"This one is different," I said. "It has a history of publishing some really good writers. I have a chance to write a story that will let millions of people know what's going on down here. That's a good thing."

"And do you think people will change their lives after reading your story? Do you really believe they'll do anything to make things better?"

"I don't know," I said, "but I take the job seriously and want to write the best story that I can."

She was not impressed, so I had to beg. I told her that I needed some help, that I didn't speak Spanish very well, and that I really didn't have any leads for a story. I asked her if I could come to La Realidad and if she would help me interview the Zapatistas.

"I can't say whether you can come or not," she said. "It's not up to me. You'll have to get permission from the leaders."

"I've actually been to La Realidad once already," I said, "and it was kind of hard to get back out. Maybe I could get a ride with you?"

"I'm going back this afternoon, but you'll have to find your own ride. If you can get there and get permission, I'll help you, but only if you get permission."

I'd been sent to Chiapas to try to get an interview with the mysterious and charismatic Subcommander Marcos. It was Marcos who had read the Zapatista Declaration of War from the second-story balcony of the presidential palace in San Cristobal on January 1, 1994. He was quick witted and spoke from his heart in short, clean sound bites. He'd joked with the press, saying that he had taken the exam to be a full commander, but that he'd failed the part on press relations. He was asked, "Why the masks?" and he said that politics in Mexico was "a culture of coverings," and that "I am willing to take off the ski mask if Mexican society takes off the mask that the anxieties of foreign vocations have already been imposing for many years." It took a year for the government to reveal his former identity as —— Guillen. He had grown up in a middle-class suburb of Tampico, attended the Autonomous University in Mexico City where he studied philosophy and wrote his thesis on Louis Althusser, a second-generation Marxist. After graduating, Guillen spent a few years working as a professor of communications and then left the university and Mexico City altogether, in 1983, to go live among the Indians in the Lacandon jungle, near the border of Chiapas and Guatemala. There he joined the incipient EZLN, or the Zapatista Liberation Forces, and worked his way up through the ranks to become their chief military strategist.

I arrived in San Cristobal two days before the conference, or "Encuentro," was to begin, which I considered to be a stroke of luck, as I hadn't known about it. I found the local stringer for the *New York Times*, and she very nicely lined me up with a video news crew that was driving into the jungle to document the Zapatista leaders, coming out of hiding and riding under Red Cross escort back to San Cristobal. We left early the next morning, drizzling and dark—a producer, reporter, soundman, two print journalists, all from Mexico City. We rode in a Chevy Suburban, our clothes clean and pressed, ready to meet the primitives. The road began as a freeway that dropped down from the alpine hills of San Cristobal to a high plain covered by farms and ranches, and then turned onto a two-lane highway that became a dirt road that wound back up through some hills that became increasingly tropical—a place of monkeys, parrots and butterflies. The Lacandon jungle.

The others in the car ignored me. To them I was a carpetbagger. Not even the soundman would be my friend. Perhaps I ruined my chances early on in the ride when I asked the producer if he knew of any way to get an interview with Subcommander Marcos. This made everyone in the Suburban laugh.

"Marcos has done only one interview in the last two years," the producer said, "and that one was only last week, as a way of commenting on the upcoming conference. He said he will not come to the conference, as there is nothing to say until the government meets the conditions of the San Andreas Accords. He said that for now he will speak by his silence. I doubt very much that you will be able to talk to him."

We drove deep into the jungle; sometimes the road was all but washed away, sometimes it was obscured by fog. We went through small towns, some with little churches and warnings on buildings about cholera. We passed two army bases. The ride ended in La Real-idad, which served as a Zapatista base of operations.

We sat for five hours, watching big cumulus clouds build up over the mountains, and then, in the early afternoon, five hundred camp-esinos, men and women, came up the road chanting slogans, holding protest banners, and waving their hands in the air. All were disguised by bandanas or balaclavas. Through the center of this crowd emerged four small but heavily armed Zapatistas officers, also wearing black balaclavas. The media swarmed them for photos and video, and they stopped to pose before giving up their arms and getting into the Red Cross Landcruisers.

I was taking photos of the protestors when I realized that the Landcruisers and the Suburban had left the village. I asked around if there might be a taxi in town.

No, there were no taxis. There were not even any vehicles in town.

"A bus perhaps, something passing through on the highway?"

"No, nothing until next week."

"Next week?"

"Yes, next week."

I sat on the side of the road, refusing to accept that there was no one else trying to get out of the jungle, believing in the power of the road to bring a vehicle. After two hours of waiting I got a ride out with some of the people from the rally who had been masked and shouting. They came from the far side of town in a long line of two-ton cargo trucks, each so tightly packed that there were men on top of the cab and also perched along the high wooden sidewalls around the bed. It started to rain, and it rained hard for five hours of the six-hour drive out of the jungle. I was freezing, my hands were blue, but the others didn't seem to notice. They were tough campesinos. What had they been shouting? That they wanted to live with dignity.

Back in San Cristobal I attended a preliminary discussion in the conference hall and was asked by a young man sitting next to me if I thought Marcos would be there. I said that I'd been told he wouldn't, and went back to trying to decipher a story in a local newpaper, only to realize, a minute later, that my backpack had been taken—the kid's question had been a diversion. I left the meeting and wandered the streets feeling really stupid. But then, the next day, I met Sarah and things seemed to be looking up again.

Back to La Realidad

I stayed in San Cristobal for the three-day conference, but nothing was accomplished by the dialogue. The Zapatistas wanted their own autonomous region with control over the water and natural resources—including natural gas, petroleum and hardwoods. The government representatives said, in effect, "Yes, we understand but these things are very difficult, perhaps impossible at this time . . ." then they left town in their limousines and private jets.

I caught a series of rides back to the jungle, beginning in a Volkswagen bus with commuters on their way to work and ending in the back of a cargo truck with six Mayan Indians, wearing irrigation boots and soccer cleats, pants with broken zippers, collar shirts open down their chests, and beat-up straw cowboy hats. They spoke Tojolabal, and when they laughed I saw their teeth were capped with gold.

The truck stopped and I got out on the edge of La Realidad. I told the men who checked my papers, "I have a letter to the comandancia, asking for permission to conduct interviews." The three men were dressed as campesinos, but they were soldiers, and the one with the Chicago Bulls hat was the ranking officer. He read my letter and told me to wait and walked down the road into the village. He came back out on the road twenty minutes later and waved for me to come in. I was introduced to Max, the village headman, leaning in the doorway of a long building, holding my letter in his hand.

"You can wait here," he said, pointing inside. It was a storehouse, empty except for some wooden benches and some bags of mortar. "I'll send your message to the comandancia. You can go to the river," he said, pointing to a stream only thirty yards away, "but do not cross the bridge. You can cross the road," pointing in the opposite direction, "and go to the store to buy drinks and crackers. My house is just beyond the store, and my wife can prepare your meals. Don't go beyond my house. Stay between it and the river. Do you understand me?"

"Yes, certainly. Are the commanders in the area?"

"They live in the jungle," he said, making a sweeping motion with his arm.

"In the area?"

"Yes, in the area," he said in a way that could mean anywhere from three miles to one hundred miles away.

"How long do you think it will it take for permission to come?"

"How long do you have?"

"A few days, a week."

"It's possible for it to return in four to six days, but then it's possible that it will take longer. And even then they may say no."

I sat on the porch of the storehouse and waited. In front was a village green, a common area with grass, some children pounding aluminum cans on a stack of adobe bricks, a little girl in a pink dress carrying a baby on her back and walking barefoot back and forth through a mud puddle, singing. Across the stream was a huge old ceiba tree, eighty feet tall and one hundred feet wide, with big leaves and parrots flying in and out. Beside the tree was a soccer goal—one end of a soccer field that I couldn't see because the ground sloped away. Above the soccer goal on a small hill was a house with a mural of Emiliano Zapata painted across its backside. Opposite this mural, on the other end of the green, was the church, and just next to the church was another mural, this one showing the masked faces of four Zapatista military leaders, one of whom was Subcommander Marcos—the one with the pipe.

I watched a young mother washing clothes in the stream beside the bridge. She scrubbed them on a rock on the shore, rinsed a couple of times, wrung them hard, and hung them along a barbed wire fence in the sun to dry. When she was done with the clothes she poured some water over the head of her young daughter, who'd been playing naked in the water, and then scrubbed her hair with the same soap she'd used to wash the clothes. The girl rubbed her eyes and cried softly. Then the mother took off her blouse and washed her own hair, not caring that I was there. I couldn't help admiring her breasts, which were brown and beautiful.

She was an Indian and I was an idiot.

It rained all night in spurts, sounding like a hundred marimba players on the tin roof of the storehouse, and then stopping altogether, and then starting again, over and over. At six A.M., when it was just starting to get light, I peeked out of my sleeping bag on the porch and saw there was a thick fog on the ground. I went back to sleep. A few minutes later I heard soft voices and looked and saw, through the fog, seven men standing on the grass with long machetes in their hands. I went back to sleep and woke a few minutes later when one of the men, a young man, sat down beside me on the wooden bench and started sharpening his blade in slow careful strokes. I sat up in my bag. He didn't say hello. I didn't say hello. It was too early to say hello. Soon sixty men were standing in a circle on the grass, all with machetes, speaking Tojolabal or Tzetsil or who knows what—a language where many words are spoken through the teeth. It started to drizzle. One man stepped into the center of the circle. They were trying to figure out where and how to go to work for the day. There seemed to be three factions. I had no real idea of what they were saying, so I made it up:

"You want to burn your field but it is raining now and it will rain all day!"

"The sun is coming! We can cut in the morning and burn in the afternoon!"

"I have forty coffee trees ready to harvest!"

"My brother is leaving for the city and will take all bags to the market, but we need to bring them to his house!"

"Last time your brother went to town he didn't come back for a week!"

"Or your sister!"

"Today is the day for digging ditches, my friends, today is the day for building fences!"

The man in the center of the circle, fielding arguments from all sides, turned around and around, speaking forcefully, then loudly, then with some frustration, and finally throwing up his hands and walking back into the circle, whereupon it split into three different groups that walked away in separate directions, all disappearing in the fog.

I saw Sarah again in the afternoon when the Mexican Army convoy came through town. I heard the engines coming up the road, slowly—a tank, followed by thirty-five Humvees, each with a big machine gun mounted on top and six men in combat gear inside. Sarah and the other observers came over the bridge from their house near the soccer field and stood on the road with notebooks and video cameras. Some of the men in the convoy, in return, had their own notebooks and video cameras, and as they passed by there was a great burst of documentation.

When the convoy had gone, Sarah came over to the storehouse where I was sitting. She was carrying a little girl—her arms around Sarah's neck and her cheek pressed against Sarah's chest.

"You made it," she said, as if she wasn't real glad to see me.

"Yeah, but I'm waiting for permission. What's with all the cameras?"

She put the little girl down and took a pipe out of her pocket and lit it. It looked kind of silly, as if she was trying to be like Subcommander Marcos.

"That's why we're here," she said. "Or it's at least a part of why we're here. It's so they know that we know who they are. So they can't kill with impunity. Kill whoever for whatever reason and nobody ever knows, which was standard practice in Guatemala and El Salvador, and would be here as well."

"And why do the Mexican soldiers photograph you?"

"Intimidation. To let us know they can kick us out any time. Because last year Mexico passed a new law making it illegal for foreigners with tourist visas to participate in political events, or to be political in any way. They've expelled a hundred and fifty observers this year."

"But you *are* political in a lot of ways."

"No we're not," she said, suddenly angry. "We stay out of the decision-making process completely. What the people in this village do is entirely their own choice. We help them pick coffee. We help them build their health clinic."

"But you sit here and keep the Mexican government from carrying out a war, a war that was declared and enacted upon them. You help the enemy."

"What is it you're after?" she said.

"I'm just trying to figure things out."

"Well, I can't help you," she said. "I don't like journalists. I don't like the whole idea of journalism. There've been lots of reporters who've come here trying to get interviews with the commanders, and they're all the same. All they want is a quick story and then they leave. They don't care at all about the people here. All they care about is themselves and their egos."

I told her that I didn't like journalists either, and that I'd never really considered myself to be one. "I try to write what I see," I said. "I don't know what else I can do. And as far as not caring for these people, I mean, I've been here a few days and I can't talk to anyone. I need some help."

"Well, you'll have to find some other way," she said. "I really shouldn't be talking to you at all." Then she picked up the little girl and walked away.

She was a tough nut to crack. She'd been to school and had studied feminism and Marxism and saw me as an agent of the dominant ideology, which I considered to be a lot of naive, guilt-ridden, dualistic crap. But then there was the fact that the magazine I worked for was founded by William Randolph Hearst, who had been an enemy of Emiliano Zapata and Pancho Villa. During the Mexican Revolution of 1910–1919 Hearst had tried to convince the U.S. government to invade Mexico and take it as a colony. His father, George, had made his fortune by acquiring mines on lands that had been given to and then taken back from Native Americans—in Colorado, from the Utes, and in the Black Hills, from the Sioux, and then in Mexico, from the Commanches and other tribes farther south. It was this kind of behavior, between men like George Hearst and Mexican president Porfirio Díaz, that had led the original Zapatistas and Villistas to rise up in rebellion and fight for agrarian reform.

I tried to believe that this didn't matter now; that it was all water under the bridge. I tried to tell myself that it made no difference that the magazine was still owned by Hearst's family, and that my paychecks came from their corporation. I thought that with enough time I could show Sarah that my intentions were good. And then I thought I was actually full of shit, and that I'd been busted by a young beauty who saw that I was, after all, just like all the others.

Every day I sat and waited. Every night the frogs would sound like jackhammers or, if I stretched it, like machine-gun fire. Every night I was wounded by fleas that fed on my flesh. I knew that this was not enough in the way of blood and guts to satisfy my editors—that just sitting, looking at the bush, so many shades of green, so vibrant, was not part of my job. And I thought there was a good possibility that Max had crumpled up my letter of request the minute he left me there. Either that or he had put it in a collection of similar letters—something he was working on for a book.

Every day the oldest man in the village came by to talk and smoke my Marlboro cigarettes. He walked with the help of a long stick, a staff, as he had an old wound on his left shin from an accident with an axe. The skin around the wound was white, and beyond that, black, maybe gangrenous. We had conversations where neither of us understood what the other was saying.

"The name of this town is 'The Reality,' but the reality of what?"
I asked.

"Chickens," he said.

"Chickens?"

"Yes."

"The reality of chickens?"

"Yes, of chickens."

I also slowly met the other foreign observers, who would come by, one or two at a time, to talk and try to relieve some of their boredom, which seemed to be the most difficult part of their job. There was Ortzi, a twenty-year-old Basque whose father was in jail in Spain for subversion, but all his aunts and uncles were acrobats for Barnum and Bailey. There was nineteen-year-old Alexander and his girlfriend, who asked me if I had any Pixies tapes. They were upper-middle-class university students from Mexico City studying social anthropology. Alexander said his parents had been radicals when they were younger but had gone soft in their old age. He swore he'd never stop fighting for the campesinos.

Then there was Pepe, a big and boisterous Italian who I once saw wearing a yellow bath towel, toga-style, strutting about like a rooster, singing love songs. And Gabriel, a small, thin Italian who had suffered a collapsed colon and had been taken to a new government health clinic nearby, only to be told that there were no doctors, not even any nurses, and that there had never been any doctors or nurses and probably never would be any doctors and nurses. So they drove him over the road out of the jungle to a hospital where his large intestine was cut and spliced back together. He never even went home to Italy to recover.

And then there was Pedro, who was, at thirty-three, the elder in the group. He was from southern France, and said he'd grown up with a lot of people whose families had been refugees from the Spanish Revolution of 1936 to 1939. "They gave their lives for three years," he told me, "and they would have done it all over again. They said, 'Yes we lost, but someday we will win.' These people were my teachers."

Pedro told me he had stood in front of machine guns on three occasions, preventing the murder of campesinos by the Mexican military. He'd been in Guatemala in the late 1980s, and he told me how things were different in Chiapas. "In Guatemala," he said, "the insurgents did not protect their villages. Here we have learned how to make war while protecting the villages. One hundred thousand people died in Guatemala, and their rebel forces were the best soldiers of the jungle, but the military destroyed their villages and killed the village people, and so the soldiers, the rebel army, were destroyed as well. But here . . . in 1995, one year after the uprising, the Mexican army attacked by land and by air, trying to kill the leaders, but the people fled into the jungle, and when the helicopters came they had only chickens to shoot at. The people stayed in the jungle for two months, until the army retreated."

"So they can live in the jungle without support?"

"They have support," he said. "They have many small fields scattered everywhere, with trails in between that only they know about. They make booby traps—trees and branches that explode when you walk by. The army has the roads, but the Zapatistas have the jungle."

"So, what do you think will happen here?" I asked. "If the government can't win a war with the Zapatistas, then don't they either have to negotiate or buy them off somehow?"

"The Zapatistas will not be bought off," he said. "I am certain that they will not be bought. But as for what might happen, I have many questions, and no answers."

Sarah spent her days in the fields, helping to pick coffee, which was the primary cash crop in the area. I suppose she'd decided that I wasn't so bad, or maybe that she'd been overly harsh with me, because she'd come by to see me sometimes after work—her T-shirt and sweatpants all wet and dirty and clinging to her body, and I would wait all day just to see her.

We had strange conversations where she would sort of open up and tell me about herself, and then I would make some comment that she interpreted as being political or judgmental and she'd become hostile. She told me about her boyfriend back in Oregon who was twice her age and married and how difficult the relationship was, and I said, "Well, what do you expect?" She told me how she planned to spend ten years in Mexico, helping the poor, and I said that seemed a little unrealistic and that she was maybe setting her goals too high, which upset her. She said she had studied Buddhism and had decided to live as a bodhisattva, which was someone who had dedicated him- or herself to do whatever it took, over countless lifetimes, to attain perfect enlightenment in order to save all beings from suffering. I asked her why she'd come to Chiapas in the first place.

"I was in a rich white girls' school in Oaxaca," she said, "a transfer program, studying Spanish and writing about Buddhism in Mexico. I read about the Zapatistas on the Internet and saw there was a need for observers. So I came here and volunteered because I believed in their cause and how they were fighting for equal rights. I came and stayed three months last year, and then went back home for a semester at the University of Oregon."

"And did it change you, being down here?"

"I'm not sure how I changed, but I must have because when I went back I had sort of a nervous breakdown. I enrolled in a bunch of classes. I dedicated all my schooltime to learning about Latin American politics and history, and the U.S. impact on Latin American politics and history—you know, how we've been raping and pillaging since Teddy Roosevelt, that big fat asshole with that big fat stick.

"As it turned out, it was too much to absorb. I don't know if it was the classes themselves or the information, but I didn't finish the semester. I just fell apart. For two months I was afraid to leave my house. I didn't want to live, I didn't want to die. It all just seemed so futile. And it still does seem so futile. I just don't think we should be comfortable watching television, while the rest of the world doesn't have food and shelter and education.

"I remember standing out in the street in front of my house, watching a Frito Lay truck come at me and not even caring if it hit me. So I came back here, because I knew I loved these people. I hate America. I hate every stitch in the goddamn flag."

"What about Oregon?" I asked. "Don't you love the sky and the mountains in Oregon?"

"Yeah," she said, "Oregon is the most beautiful place in the world. I just don't think I can live there anymore."

I could have labeled her as bipolar, or manic-depressive, or schizophrenic, and I don't think I would have been wrong. But, for some reason, I completely identified with what she was saying. I mean she was young, only twenty-three, and she had grown up in "the land of the free and the home of the brave" only to realize that it was all bullshit. She was, in this way, simply too exposed, too raw for her own good, and she was caught trying to come to terms with the big lies of our culture. She made me remember that I too hated America, every stitch in the goddamn flag.

Late at night on the sixth day Max came by to see me. He said there would be no interview with the commanders. I asked him if the commanders had said no, or whether there had been no reply, and he just shook his head. "Now is not a good time," he said. "Maybe if you could come back next year." I left the next morning on a cargo truck, Sarah standing in the road crying.

1997 the Chase

On a Sunday in July I'm eating dinner at my mother's house, and I mention to my brother that Creighton and I are going out to the desert, west of the Great Salt Lake, to try chasing antelope again. I tell him that Creighton was inspired by the Seri, that he's been running a lot since we got back, and I'd feel like a flake if I didn't go with him. I tell my brother this without any conviction, without expecting him to be interested. But to my surprise he is interested. He says he wants to go.

"I had other plans but I'll change them." He seems a little upset that I didn't expect him to go.

"Yeah, O.K.," I say. "Good. Let's do it."

There are five of us: my brother, Creighton, myself, and our friends Calvin and Brian, who are also excellent runners. We're camped on a hillside overlooking Puddle Valley—a basin ten miles in diameter, not a tree in sight, and ringed by small barren mountains. It's 2:00 P.M. and one hundred degrees and we're trying to decide on a strategy. Creighton and I know how the Seri chased deer; they told us how they did it through a series of heats. But neither of us brings it up, now that we could use it. Somehow it doesn't seem to apply here. Also, my brother is worried about catching the attention of one of the many possible federal agents in the area. We are right next to a bombing range. He's coming up for tenure shortly. How would he explain this illegal hunt to his review committee?

What we end up doing is this: we get in two cars and drive down the road and find the Lone Male standing there waiting for us. We drive by like we are not interested. We stop about a mile away and get out and argue some more about how we are going to do this. Then we get back in the cars and drive back to the Lone Male, who is still waiting for us. Then we pile out of the cars and start chasing him.

He runs due west and we spread out in a long line that quickly becomes a vee. Creighton is a much faster runner and is out in the lead; my brother is a ways behind him; and I'm running north, hoping that the antelope will turn clockwise and I'll be able to cut him off.

I run and sometimes stop to look and see the antelope and Creighton—tiny blurs slowly moving on the surface of a mirage. I see my brother, a blur behind. I run and stop and don't see anything. I take out my binoculars and look around and finally see a white blur going north—the ass of the Lone Male. I scan to the south and see Creighton, a small beetle, in pursuit.

They're heading north so I turn east and run about a half-hour and I come back to the road. I stop and look around, seeing my truck two miles down the road, but no antelope, no people. I stand there a little while and wait, wondering what to do. Just as I think I've blown it, the Lone Male comes over a rise right in front of me. What a rush! He sees me and runs over the road and into a sand wash, and quickly all I'm seeing is his tail again. I start after it, realizing that the others are far away and it's up to me now. The antelope has run for almost an hour and covered maybe twenty miles in one-hundred-degree heat. I've run maybe a quarter of that distance, and I have water on my back that I've been drinking the whole time. If there is any human advantage, like my brother thought there might be, I should certainly have it now. I run thinking, "This is it. He did just what I thought he would. This is the whole thing right now." And I laugh. I laugh and run and it is, for sure, the best thing I've ever done. I have everything I need, the wilderness is unfolding in front of me.

acknowledgments

Many of the stories in this book were originally written and produced for broadcast on public radio with funds provided by the Corporation for Public Broadcasting and the National Endowment for the Arts. I say this not to fulfill any contractual obligation, but out of respect for a system of public support for the arts and sciences. Besides this, there is a long list of individuals who have helped me over the years, and I'm glad to finally have some space to thank them.

In 1983 Alex Chadwick let me in the door and helped me produce my first stories at National Public Radio in Washington, D.C. During that time Larry Massett, Joe Frank, Madeleine Lundberg, and Art Silverman loaned me money, let me crash at their homes, and also showed me how to be an independent producer.

In 1994 I started writing stories for Ira Glass and "This American Life" from WBEZ in Chicago. Ira's editing skills and keen sense of radio were a tremendous help to me, although much of what I wrote for his show was done in order to please his associate producer, Alix Spiegel, who had rather high standards.

From Ira's show I started getting offers from magazines, most importantly from *Esquire*, where Andy Ward was patient enough to read draft after draft of my stories, and David Granger boldly sent me to the other side of the planet.

As for this collection, I got the idea of how to put it together from reading Charles Bowden, the best non-fiction writer in the country. My agent, Kathy Anderson, was smart enough to offer the work to Counterpoint, where Dawn Seferian accepted what was a rather sloppy manuscript and then insisted that I make it into something that I am proud of.

And then there are my friends, all of whom have waited a couple of decades for this physical proof of my alleged efforts—Beth Burckhardt, Trent and Jeffrey Harris, Kenny Larsen, Calvin Lloyd, Barrett Golding, Alex Caldiero, Joe Pachak, Creighton King, Terry Tempest Williams, Doug Peacock, Dennis Sizemore, and Ned Judge.

This leaves my family, who saw everything, endured everything, and never doubted that things would work out fine.